Don't Suspend Me!

Second Edition

This book is dedicated to all students at a crossroads in their educational career and/or life, where the path they take will be determined by the decisions educators and administrators make—who either support by teaching behavior or reject by using traditional exclusionary methods. May this book help educators return a student to their correct path where they will have the opportunities to reach their dreams because they were supported behaviorally.

Don't Suspend Me!

An Alternative Discipline Toolkit

Second Edition

Jessica Djabrayan Hannigan

John E. Hannigan

FOR INFORMATION:

Corwin

A SAGE Company

2455 Teller Road

Thousand Oaks, California 91320

(800) 233-9936

www.corwin.com

SAGE Publications Ltd.

1 Oliver's Yard

55 City Road

London EC1Y 1SP

United Kingdom

SAGE Publications India Pvt. Ltd.

B 1/I 1 Mohan Cooperative Industrial Area

Mathura Road, New Delhi 110 044

India

SAGE Publications Asia-Pacific Pte. Ltd.

18 Cross Street #10-10/11/12

China Square Central

Singapore 048423

President: Mike Soules

Vice President and Editorial Director: Monica Eckman

Publisher: Jessica Allan

Senior Content Development Editor: Lucas Schleicher

Associate Content Development Editor: Mia Rodriguez

Editorial Assistant: Natalie Delpino

Production Editor: Tori Mirsadjadi

Copy Editor: Terri Lee Paulsen

Typesetter: C&M Digitals (P) Ltd.

Cover Designer: Candice Harman

Marketing Manager: Olivia Bartlett

Toolkit icons courtesy of iStock.com/musmellow.

Note From the Publisher: The authors have provided content in the book that is available to you through QR (quick response) codes. To read a QR code, you must have a smartphone or tablet with a camera. We recommend that you download a QR code reader app that is made specifically for your phone or tablet brand.

Printed in the United States of America

Library of Congress Cataloging-in-Publication Data

Names: Djabrayan Hannigan, Jessica, author. | Hannigan, John E., author.

Title: Don't suspend me! : an alternative discipline toolkit / Jessica Djabrayan Hannigan, John E. Hannigan.

Description: Second edition. | Thousand Oaks, California : Corwin, [2022] | Includes bibliographical references and index.

Identifiers: LCCN 2022004729 | ISBN 9781071870143 (paperback) | ISBN 9781071870150 (epub) | ISBN 9781071870136 (epub) | ISBN 9781071870129 (pdf)

Subjects: LCSH: Rewards and punishments in education. | School discipline. | Problem children—Behavior modification.

Classification: LCC LB3025 .D53 2022 | DDC 371.5—dc23

LC record available at https://lccn.loc.gov/2022004729

This book is printed on acid-free paper.

22 23 24 25 26 10 9 8 7 6 5 4 3 2 1

Contents

Preface

THE SCHOOL SYSTEM WILL SUPPORT ALL STUDENTS WITH . . .
OUR SCHOOL EXISTS TO PROVIDE ALL STUDENTS A . . .
. . . WHERE THE CHILD COMES FIRST.

You can probably finish the rest of these school or district mission or vision statements, but can you finish them while confidently including the importance of the social-emotional needs of *all* students? To advocate for *all* students when using discipline in an alternative fashion, these commonly used mission or vision statements need to include, ". . . the social-emotional learning of a student is valued as importantly as any academic subject taught in school." Most mission and vision statements say we support *all* students, but do our actions reflect it when it comes to student behavior? Can we support equity for all students and focus on the social-emotional development of a student while using punitive, exclusionary practices as the only means of teaching behavior? Additionally, there is disproportionality in discipline for students of color when compared to their white counterparts for similar behavior incidents in schools. For there to be equity in school discipline, a belief system is needed that allows educators to advocate for individualized responses to student behavior rather than a one-size-fits-all approach.

We understand the challenge of looking at behavior in the ways described in this book. This book is not based on theory; it is written by practitioners for practitioners and is based on our experiences in changing behavior by using alternatives. The at-risk behavior students on your campus are at a crossroads that will define the direction of their lives. Therefore, the need for innovative methods for addressing discipline is now. Misconceptions arise when the term *alternative discipline* is mentioned; some think of alternative discipline as an excuse to dismiss poor behavior. This is not what is meant by alternative discipline. To help clarify, you need to know what alternative discipline is not.

Alternative discipline is not stopping the suspension of students in order to meet a school or district behavior data quota.

It is using other means of discipline to help students learn from their behaviors rather than sending them home as the first response.

Alternative discipline is not ignoring the stakeholders who have been affected by the student's behavior.

It is working with the stakeholders to help restore what has been damaged and work together to help the student change their behavior.

Alternative discipline is not assigning the same discipline for every student without knowing the reason for the misbehavior.

It is taking the time to learn about what triggered the behavior in the first place.

Alternative discipline is not a school that does not have effective behavior systems (foundation) in place to support responding to discipline in this fashion.

It is how discipline is handled in a school that has systems of behavioral supports in place for school-wide, targeted/at-risk groups, and individualized students (special education and general education).

Alternative discipline is not assigned without consistent implementation and follow-through.

It is a method of delivery that requires the administrator and stakeholders to work together and ensure all components of the alternative discipline are put into place and implemented with fidelity.

Alternative discipline is not easy to do.

It is time intensive and requires a belief system in the leader(s) of the school and/or district to create a culture that supports working with students in this fashion.

This book is written to encourage educators to look at discipline from a unique lens. Issues with discipline and challenging behaviors in school tend to provoke negative feelings from educators. We want to help educators take a minute to reflect on what makes discipline frustrating and difficult for stakeholders and feel comfortable with approaching discipline in the way we are suggesting. In order to do so, a school system needs to have a healthy functioning behavioral/social-emotional system designed to respond to the behavioral needs of *all* students. Approaching discipline by only using the traditional approach of suspension is not working for *all* students. Therefore, we challenge educators to be aware of the misconceptions of alternative discipline and really own the words designed to frame a school's or district's identity and culture.

Acknowledgments

We wish to personally thank all schools and districts across the nation we have trained to utilize alternative discipline methods. Also, to all of our supervisors, mentors, professors, colleagues, students, friends, and family who have allowed us to innovate and shared in our passion for what we believe in. This would not have been possible without all of you.

To the Djabrayan and Hannigan families, we thank you for your endless love, support, and encouragement. A special thank-you to our parents, Bedros and Dzovinar Djabrayan and Mike and Sky Hannigan, for your help and relentless support during this process.

To our amazing children, John John, Riley, and Rowan, thank you for all your love and support and for always being our number one fans. Through this book, we hope to model for you what it means to set high goals and never give up.

Our appreciation goes to the team at Corwin for recognizing this is a comprehensive and innovative method of addressing and supporting student behaviors. Thank you for giving us the platform to share our voice and help students.

To all who read this book, we thank you for truly doing what is best for *all* students.

About the Authors

Dr. Jessica Djabrayan Hannigan is an assistant professor in the Educational Leadership Department at California State University, Fresno. She works with schools and districts throughout the nation on designing and implementing effective behavior systems. Her expertise includes Response to Intervention (RTI) Behavior, Multi-Tiered System of Supports (MTSS), Positive Behavior Interventions and Supports (PBIS), Social and Emotional Learning (SEL), and more. The combination of her special education and student support services background, school and district-level administration, and higher education research experiences has allowed her to develop inclusive research-based best practices around systemic implementation of behavior initiatives throughout the nation. She is the coauthor of the following educational books: *The PBIS Tier One Handbook, The PBIS Tier Two Handbook, The PBIS Tier Three Handbook, Building Behavior, The MTSS Start-Up Guide,* and *Behavior Solutions, SEL From a Distance,* and the first edition of *Don't Suspend Me!* Some of her recognitions include being named California Outstanding School Psychologist of the Year, Administrator of the Year, and Outstanding Faculty Publications and Service Award recipient; being recognized by the California Legislature Assembly for her work in social justice and equity; and receiving the inaugural Association of California School Administrators Exemplary Woman in Education Award in 2017 for her relentless work around equity in schools.

Connect with her on Twitter @Jess_hannigan

Dr. John Hannigan has served in education for over 20 years as a teacher, instructional coach, principal, and county office leadership coach. John is a sought-after consultant who works with schools and districts throughout North America on designing and implementing systematic multi-tiered systems of support for academics and behavior.

During his nine years as principal of Reagan Elementary in California's Sanger Unified School District, it earned California State Distinguished School, California Title I Academic Achievement Award, Gold Ribbon School, California Honor Roll School, Bonner Award for Character Education, and Platinum Level Model School Recognition for positive behavior interventions and supports.

John has written numerous articles, coauthored nine books, and is the cofounder of Hannigan Ed-Equity Group LLC.

John holds a doctorate in educational leadership from California State University, Fresno.

Connect with him on Twitter @JohnHannigan75

Introduction to the Second Edition

The first edition of this book began with a quote: "A student struggling to read is not sent home and expected to return reading fluently, so why is it that a student struggling to behave is sent home and expected to return behaving decently?" This quote continues to guide our work in schools today. Since the publication of the first edition in 2017, we have presented and provided professional learning to thousands of educators throughout the nation to disrupt the inequities in school discipline. Schools have made tremendous progress changing the narrative of school discipline through this work but have been thrown a serious curveball with the COVID-19 pandemic shifting the priority structures in schools. As students returned to in-person instruction, their behavioral needs have intensified; the impact of trauma from the pandemic (isolation, loss of loved ones, parent loss of employment, increase of domestic violence and substance abuse) on students and teachers, as well as the increase in educator burnout, has resulted in some schools reverting back to traditional, exclusionary practices.

We felt an urgency to write this book to provide encouragement to continue this essential work now more than ever. We believe this work is about saving lives and communities and therefore needs to remain a priority. This second edition includes additional lessons learned from our implementation of this work over the years, strategies to increase ownership among staff, and over 25 additional alternative discipline forms and strategies.

PART 1

The What and Why of Alternative Discipline That Works!

1

Building a Case for Alternative Discipline

"A student struggling to read is not sent home and expected to return reading fluently, so why is it that a student struggling to behave is sent home and expected to return behaving decently?"

The first known use and origin of the word *discipline* dates back to the 13th century from the Latin word *disciplina*, meaning teaching and learning. Today, some define discipline as training that corrects, molds, or perfects the mental faculties or moral character; others define discipline as a verb that means to punish in order to gain control or enforce obedience. While many would disagree on the meaning and purpose of discipline, it remains one of the most commonly stated reasons for not having enough time for effective implementation of school or classroom programs/ initiatives. While true, however, using a reactive discipline approach actually takes more time in the long run than a preventive approach. Effective discipline should be designed to improve behavior, rather than dismissing it for a few days through suspension and hoping the student returns to school "fixed." This requires thinking beyond the traditional method of sending students home and hoping that either (a) their parents will teach them not to do it again, or (b) being home from school will teach them not to do it again. In fact, the research demonstrates the contrary. We will begin making our case by comparing the evolution of both academic and behavior systems in schools.

Prior to the Individuals with Disabilities Education Act (IDEA) of 2004, the traditional method of deciding whether a struggling student receives extra time and support through special education was with the *discrepancy model*. Under the discrepancy model, action would not take place until there was a discrepancy between a student's expected achievement and their actual achievement. Simply put, a school had to wait for a student to fail before providing the supports necessary to accelerate learning. Under this model, as McCook (2006, p. 1) states, "It must be the child's fault, or the problem certainly must be the child. Why else would the child have such a discrepancy between expected achievement and actual achievement?" The "wait to fail" model produced a large number of students misidentified as requiring special education services and a disproportionate number of racial minority students misdiagnosed with a learning disability. The introduction of 2004 IDEA allowed schools to use the response to intervention (RTI) framework for identification purposes, which means only after students have failed responding to a series of timely, systematic, increasingly focused, and intensive research-based interventions will a student be considered for special education services. RTI allows schools to identify the kinds of support struggling students need and provide individualized support when it's needed.

Exclusionary discipline practices are equivalent to using the wait-to-fail approach in academics; both are reactionary, not preventive. Having an effective system of tiered supports in place (see the *PBIS Tier 1, 2, 3 Handbook Series* [Hannigan & Hauser, 2014; Hannigan & Hannigan, 2018a, 2018b] and the book *Behavior Solutions* [Hannigan et al., 2020]) coupled with an innovative response to students who misbehave (this book) does to behavior systems what 2004 IDEA and RTI were designed to do for academic systems.

The traditional mindset about student learning shifted from being the "child's fault" in a discrepancy model toward a belief that all students can and will learn. With this belief, every resource and support is exhausted to provide a student with the resources needed to support learning. However, when it comes to behavior, do we believe that every student can and will behave? Do we exhaust every resource and provide every strategy to support a student in their behavior, or do we use suspension as our only means to "teach" a student how to behave? Using suspension is the reactive wait-to-fail model for behavior. Is behavior RTI (preventive discipline) visible on your campus? Or does your system respond to behavior today with the same approach schools responded to academics 20 years ago?

Over the past few decades, methods of disciplining K–12 students have transformed significantly when compared to traditional practices, however, still not to the level it should be. Subsequently, the 2014 data findings from the U.S. Department of Education's Office for Civil Rights on School Discipline revealed:

- African American students are suspended and expelled at three times the rate of white students. On average, 5% of white students are suspended, compared to 16% of Black students.

- Students with disabilities are more than twice as likely to receive an out-of-school suspension (13%) than students without disabilities (6%).

- More than one out of four boys of color with disabilities (served by IDEA)—and nearly one in five girls of color with disabilities—receives an out-of-school suspension (U.S. Department of Education Office for Civil Rights, 2014).

Changes in state and federal policy have necessitated shifts in methods such as corporal punishment, zero tolerance, and use of exclusionary practices such as suspensions and expulsions toward creating positive behavioral environments. In analyzing over 25 years of research on discipline approaches, researchers found that out-of-school suspension and zero-tolerance approaches to discipline do not reduce or prevent misbehavior and actually correlate with lower achievement (Irvin et al., 2004; Losen, 2011; Mayer, 1995; Skiba & Peterson, 1999; Skiba & Rausch, 2006). In fact, this form of traditional discipline does not make the school feel safer and results in negative outcomes for the child and the community (Skiba & Peterson, 1999). Similarly, Balfanz and Boccanfuso (2007) found that students who were suspended and/or expelled were more likely to be held back a grade or drop out of school. Specifically, the greatest loss of instruction due to suspensions is in middle school and in both middle school and early high school grade levels, students who get suspended are even more likely to drop out of high school compared to students who have not been suspended (Balfanz & Fox, 2014; Rumberger & Losen, 2017). Losen and Martin (2018) found students of color and students with disabilities lose far more instruction than their peers even with federal law protections in place for districts to ensure due process and prevent unjust punishment. Unfortunately, this protection/safeguard is not officially triggered until after 10 days lost, contributing to the narrative of students with disabilities losing 22 more days per 100 enrolled compared to students without disabilities even with the protection of federal law (Losen & Martin, 2018).

Furthermore, the likelihood of being involved in the juvenile justice system is increased significantly for students addressed with a traditional discipline approach (Leone et al., 2003; Wald & Losen, 2003). We often hear, "the other students can't learn with this student in my class!"; Perry and Morris (2014) found that higher levels of exclusionary discipline within schools over time generate collateral damage, negatively affecting the academic achievement of *non-suspended* students in punitive contexts. Chard et al. (1992) summarized discipline practices in education by stating that, "there is one burden that consumes more time, energy, and attention than any other . . . school discipline" (p. 19). Therefore, it is not a surprise that when problem behaviors occur in schools, common practice has been to react in a stringent manner, which has not been demonstrated to be successful for all (Chard et al., 1992).

Hattie's (2018) *Visible Learning* meta-analysis that resulted in 250+ influences on student learning reveals an effect size of –0.20 for school suspensions, which represents a negative (or reverse) effect on student learning. Of the 250+ influences, less than 5% had a negative effect and suspension is one of them.

Although there is an overwhelming abundance of evidence demonstrating the negative effects of suspension, it continues to be the most commonly used method of discipline throughout the nation. We understand choosing alternative forms of discipline will be more challenging and time-consuming in the beginning. Here are some common oppositional messages we hear as we present our approach on discipline. Do any of these messages sound familiar?

But . . .

"I had to make an example out of him."

"I don't have time to do it the other way."

"I want my teachers to know I support them."

"We need to inconvenience the parents."

"I don't want the other parents to feel that nothing was done."

"We need a break from this student."

"Alternatives require more work and are more time-consuming."

"There is no way we have the time or staffing to do this."

"Why not just suspend?"

When suspending a student (knowing full well that suspensions will not change behavior), what are the actual outcomes expected from the suspension? The statements above are excuses that dismiss a student's behavior for a few days, making it easier for the adults involved. The oppositional messages above can be grouped into three categories that "save."

The Three Saves of Suspension

Save time:

"I don't have time to do it the other way."

"There is no way we have the time or staffing to do this."

Save face:

"I don't want the other parents to feel that nothing was done."

"I want my teachers to know I support them."

"We need to inconvenience the parents."

"I had to make an example out of him."

Save energy:

"Alternatives require more work and are more time-consuming."

"We need a break from this student."

Notice how everything being "saved" is for the benefit of adults and not the students at risk of failure. Students frequently suspended have an increased likelihood of dropping out of high school; a high school dropout will earn 35 cents for every dollar a college graduate earns and 60 cents for every dollar a high school graduate earns (OECD, 2014). High school dropouts are 63 times more likely to be incarcerated

(Breslow, 2012). California, for example, is expected to spend more than $62,000 on each prison inmate—almost seven times the $9,200 it will spend for each K–12 student (Hanson & Stipek, 2014). On average, each high school dropout costs taxpayers $292,000 over that dropout's lifetime (Breslow, 2012). Furthermore, female dropouts will live an average of 10 and a half fewer years than females who graduate from college. Male dropouts will live an average of 13 fewer years than males who graduate from college (Tavernise, 2012).

Knowing the negative outcomes suspensions produce, educators still use these oppositional messages as excuses that help them save time, save face, and save energy. Discipline practices need to shift from convenience for adults to saving lives and reshaping a student's path toward a successful future.

If another opposition is that it is too time-consuming to use alternatives and easier to send a student home rather than teach them correct behavior, consider this: A typical suspension based on our collective experiences as site administrators takes approximately up to two hours of an administrator's time (interviews, investigations, paperwork, phone calls, and meeting with parents, etc.). Suspensions do not correct the behavior and will likely repeat, leading to multiple two-hour occurrences. Using the suspendable incident as a teaching opportunity will reduce the recidivism of a repeated occurrence, consequently leading to fewer suspensions and significantly decreasing the amount of time spent disciplining. The Time Cost of Suspension visual below is an example of the cost of 30 suspensions a year or 50 suspensions a year at a school on administrators, teachers, and students. For the case of this example, let's assume the average suspension day per student is two days (which is typical for average days assigned to students who receive a suspension).

Time Cost of Suspension		
	30 Suspensions a Year	**50 Suspensions a Year**
Administrator Time (i.e., investigation, communication, documentation) *2 hours per suspension	60 Hours	100 Hours
Teacher Time (i.e., documentation, student work preparation) *1 hour per suspension	30 Hours	50 Hours
Student Time (i.e., instructional time lost) *2 hours from day of incident and 14 hours for 2 days of suspension on average	480 Hours	800 Hours
Totals	570 Hours	950 Hours

If preventive and effective discipline is a priority, you will make it one of the central initiatives at your school. To make this work, it is critical to intentionally create a system designed to support alternative discipline. Here are seven actions to consider to successfully make time for alternative discipline:

Communicate Beliefs about Discipline. As educators, we approach instruction with the belief that every student can and will learn. With this belief, we exhaust every resource and support necessary to improve learning. As an administrator, you have to question your own beliefs about discipline. Do you believe every student can and will behave decently? Is every resource and strategy exhausted to support a student in their behavior, or is suspension used as the only means to "teach" a student how to behave? If you believe what you are currently doing is working, there is no compelling reason to change. If you do not believe in preventive discipline, it will not be an expectation nor a priority in your school.

Invest in Preventive Response to Intervention (RTI) Systems for Both Academics and Behavior. Invest in building your school staff's understanding around creating effective systems for responding to students school-wide, targeted/at-risk groups, and individualized both in academics and behavior. Investing here will give you more time to focus on a preventive model rather than a reactive one. Initial best teaching and best classroom management will support approximately 80% of your students in both academics and behavior. It is also imperative to organize your school's targeted/at-risk and individualized interventions for students who are not responding to the school-wide approach.

Encourage Visibility and Active Supervision. As an administrator, it is critical to be out of your office and visible to students and staff to build effective relationships and make meaningful connections with students. Active supervision requires an intentional focus on movement, scanning, and positive interactions during supervision; this is essential and needs to be modeled by the administrator. Taking the time to train your staff on visibility and active supervision will save you the time of responding to behavior incidents due to deficiencies in supervision from staff.

Invest in Gaining Faculty Commitment and Ownership. Take time to educate your staff on alternative discipline approaches. Make it a priority to share school behavior data, gather input from the staff, and work with staff on discipline so they feel part of the process. Share effective discipline success stories with the staff. If you take the time to do this and make yourself available to have difficult ongoing conversations around beliefs, you will see more ownership with staff when handling minor discipline and increased buy-in on major (administrator-handled) discipline. Communication is also key for staff to understand the logic behind alternative discipline. Discipline will become a team effort in supporting a student, rather than something only executed and monitored by an administrator.

Create and Nurture a Behavior Team. It is critical for every school to have a behavior team (i.e., PBIS team, Leadership Team) designed to set behavior expectations and goals, to establish and monitor behavior interventions, and to support preventive systems work. An administrator who provides a team the opportunity to meet on a regular basis to discuss school-wide, targeted/small group, and individualized behavior data and trends will benefit. This allows for data to be used to provide interventions for students by name, by need—instead of after they've escalated to the next level of discipline. Make sure the social-emotional experts on campus, such as a school counselor or school psychologist, are an active part of the behavior team. Designate this time with your behavior team; use a monitoring tool to ensure data are used to identify and monitor the progress of focus students. The emphasis here is to get to the students before they get to you.

Create a Toolkit of Effective Discipline. Organize preventive discipline ideas in a toolkit for future reference. As you conduct discipline in this manner, you will begin using a set of actions you tend to assign; therefore, when you have another similar incident, you can reference your toolkit to help save time. The alternatives in this book are designed to give options and examples of alternative forms of discipline used to correct misbehavior. This book will change your thinking about discipline. As you see how students respond to the alternatives provided, you will begin to innovate and think of your own new methods aligned to this framework to support students.

Support a System and Philosophy for Alternatives. Make sure the alternative discipline you assign is implemented with fidelity and effectively communicated to all stakeholders. Understand that establishing this will require time and human capital to implement and monitor with success. Although it may be challenging to allocate so many resources for one student, the ultimate goal is to help the student learn and change their behavior. Without an intentional focus on alternatives, the student will continue taking away time from your staff throughout the school year with continuing behavior challenges, since the function of the student's behavior was never addressed. Teaching desired outcomes through alternatives to suspension will reduce the frequency of repeat offenses, thus creating less time dealing with discipline than using suspension alone.

2

Discipline Belief Self-Inventory

The Discipline Belief Self-Inventory will provide educators with a look into their individual beliefs about discipline. Inventory statements are derived from an analysis of administrator responses across all grade levels and a range of differences between traditional and innovative/alternative discipline beliefs and/or approaches.

WHO IS THIS SELF-INVENTORY FOR?

Educators—such as teachers, school support staff, and school- and district-level administrators—who want to create effective behavior systems in their schools can benefit from this self-inventory. This inventory can also aid future educators and leaders to reflect on their discipline beliefs.

WHY DOES THIS SELF-INVENTORY MATTER TO ME?

We have found through our research and work with practitioners the primary reason alternative discipline does not work is the beliefs of the administrator at the school or district, the person responsible for establishing the school's culture. If the leader does not believe in alternative discipline methods, they (1) will implement the discipline ineffectively, resulting in a lack of buy-in from the staff and stakeholders, and (2) cannot justify the importance for students to be given the chance to learn behaviors similar to how they learn academics. Your school or district will not succeed in supporting behavior unless your beliefs about discipline shift to support it.

WHAT ARE YOUR CURRENT BELIEFS ABOUT DISCIPLINE?

Please review the statements and rate yourself on your discipline beliefs. Please be honest in your responses. Remember, this self-inventory is anonymous and designed to serve as a reflection and self-awareness of where you currently fall in your beliefs about discipline.

Discipline Belief Self-Inventory

1. Suspensions work to change student behavior.

1	2	3	4	5
Strongly Disagree				Strongly Agree

2. Discipline should be used as a teaching opportunity.

1	2	3	4	5
Strongly Disagree				Strongly Agree

3. I prefer a black-and-white discipline handbook with exact number of days outlined for suspensions based on behavior.

1	2	3	4	5
Strongly Disagree				Strongly Agree

4. Behavior should be addressed in an individualized fashion.

1	2	3	4	5
Strongly Disagree				Strongly Agree

5. Parents need to be inconvenienced with suspensions.

1	2	3	4	5
Strongly Disagree				Strongly Agree

6. Restorative, reflective, and instructional opportunities should be part of the consequence/intervention.

1	2	3	4	5
Strongly Disagree				Strongly Agree

7. Students should be suspended when teachers or stakeholders pressure me to suspend.

1	2	3	4	5
Strongly Disagree				Strongly Agree

8. I monitor student behavior on an ongoing basis.

1	2	3	4	5
Strongly Disagree				Strongly Agree

9. I use suspension to set an example.

1	2	3	4	5
Strongly Disagree				Strongly Agree

10. I find the function of the behavior and innovate a consequence based on identified function.

1	2	3	4	5
Strongly Disagree				Strongly Agree

(Continued)

(Continued)

11. I need to be convinced to use alternative discipline approaches.

1	2	3	4	5
Strongly Disagree				Strongly Agree

12. I involve parents, teachers, and other stakeholders with the assigned discipline.

1	2	3	4	5
Strongly Disagree				Strongly Agree

13. There is not enough time to do alternative discipline.

1	2	3	4	5
Strongly Disagree				Strongly Agree

14. I establish a relationship with the student throughout the alternative discipline process.

1	2	3	4	5
Strongly Disagree				Strongly Agree

15. I avoid difficult conversations about alternative discipline decisions.

1	2	3	4	5
Strongly Disagree				Strongly Agree

16. I provide a consequence/intervention in lieu of suspension.

1	2	3	4	5
Strongly Disagree				Strongly Agree

17. I prefer to send students home instead of keeping them at school.

1	2	3	4	5
Strongly Disagree				Strongly Agree

18. I am confident enough to justify the reasoning behind using alternative discipline.

1	2	3	4	5
Strongly Disagree				Strongly Agree

19. I demonstrate support to teachers by suspending students.

1	2	3	4	5
Strongly Disagree				Strongly Agree

20. I am comfortable with my skills to build believers in alternative discipline by demonstrating positive effects of using alternatives.

1	2	3	4	5
Strongly Disagree				Strongly Agree

DISCIPLINE BELIEF
SELF-INVENTORY SCORING

Scoring Note: If the combination of your odd and even point ranges do not fall into a disciplinarian category, please consider the following: (a) retake the inventory to make sure you are not contradicting yourself in your ratings, or (b) consider yourself in the emergent range due to the similarity of your scores supporting both traditional and innovative discipline beliefs.

Total odd questions: _____ Total even questions: _____

Traditional Disciplinarian: A traditional disciplinarian is a disciplinarian who prefers the black-and-white discipline handbook as a guide to how to conduct discipline. This type of disciplinarian believes this form of discipline works and prefers taking the safe route with a business-as-usual approach to discipline.

> *Total odd questions in the 40- to 50-point range **and** Total even questions in the 10- to 20-point range*

Emergent Disciplinarian: An emergent disciplinarian is inconsistent with his/her discipline practices. This type of disciplinarian assigns discipline based on his/her disposition and/or pressures from others. This type of disciplinarian does not have a strong belief about discipline one way or another. An emergent disciplinarian will experiment with alternative discipline methods but does not have the skill set or tools to do so. This usually results in using alternatives ineffectively.

> *Total odd questions in the 21- to 39-point range **and** Total even questions in the 21- to 39-point range*

Innovative Disciplinarian: An innovative disciplinarian believes in teaching behavior similar to teaching academics. This type of disciplinarian will innovate based on discipline incidents and takes the time to assign, implement, and monitor effective discipline. This type of disciplinarian is confident in having difficult conversations about behavior and has the ability to work with stakeholders on an appropriate assignment of discipline that addresses the behavior. This type of disciplinarian uses alternative discipline for every suspendable incident.

> *Total odd questions in the 10- to 20-point range **and** Total even questions in the 40- to 50-point range*

*Discipline Belief Self-Inventory Electronic Version

Type the code **bit.ly/DisciplineBeliefSelf-Inventory** into a browser to take the electronic version of the Discipline Belief Self-Inventory. You will receive a completion email after taking the survey online and will be able to download a PDF version of your responses for your records.

To read a QR code, you must have a smartphone or tablet with a camera. We recommend that you download a QR code reader app that is made specifically for your phone or tablet brand.

AUTHORS' NOTE

If you scored in the innovative disciplinarian range, you are in a solid place to begin the alternative discipline work in this book. This is the ideal range for educators to build ownership across their campus and innovate this work. If you scored in the emergent disciplinarian range, we encourage you to reflect on the components keeping you from fully embracing alternative discipline for all suspendable incidents. Our cautionary note for educators scoring in this range is the trap of inconsistent implementation (i.e., using alternative discipline for some suspendable incidents, but not others) tends to impact equity, culture, and effectiveness of implementation. If you scored in the traditional disciplinarian range, we respect your beliefs but encourage you to consider the case we put forward in Chapter 1 and revisit the more than 25 years of research that illustrate the damaging impact suspensions have on students. Suspensions are the only facet of a child's education that rests in the hands of one person, the administrator. The administrator is the gatekeeper of choosing a path where a student has the opportunity to learn from their mistakes or is sent home on a suspension knowing the detrimental impact it has on the future life trajectory of a student.

Additionally, we often see educators in this range utilize both the suspension *and* the alternative discipline concurrently, which defeats the purpose of our work. **We wrote this book to provide educators a framework for other means of correction (alternative discipline) in lieu of the suspension, not in addition to the suspension.** In the next section, we delve deeper into the work necessary to shift from traditional to innovative beliefs about discipline.

Shifting From Traditional to Innovative Belief Systems About Discipline

Shifting the traditional mindset about school discipline remains to be the number one barrier for effectively implementing alternative discipline in schools. In the second edition of this book we wanted to expand on this difficult topic. Specifically, we are concerned with the dichotomy of some educators declaring the importance of equity, inclusivity, and belonging for every student, however reverting to exclusionary practices as their response to misbehavior. How do we expect students to grow and learn from their mistakes if we do not give them the opportunities to do so?

As we think about traditional discipline beliefs, we need to identify the basis for holding onto these disproven practices. Do we discipline the way we were disciplined in our youth or witnessed others being disciplined in school? Is the function fear, control, power, safety, or support? Read the traditional discipline statements (these are actual comments we have received in our experiences training schools across the country) and use these three prompts to reflect on each statement:

1) Do you agree with the statement?

2) Why do you think the educator feels this way?

3) What would be your response to help shift their thinking?

Traditional Discipline Statements (*Note: We are highlighting these statements because we assure you, you will be hearing them or a variation of them as you do this work*):

- *To protect other students, I guess we could make them president of the student body. That makes as much sense as no suspensions.*

- *It depends on what they did. Sometimes they need to go home and think about it, and sometimes they need to go home to protect others.*

- *If the student is fighting, they need to go. The child is angry and worked up. They need time to cool for a day without hurting the staff or students.*

- *Kids think they can do whatever they want and get away with it. Disrespectful brats.*

- *What can't be tolerated is the lack of respect the students have for authority. Let's enforce some zero tolerance on these students instead of making money on high attendance.*

- *I wonder why schools are out of control. No corporal punishment, no suspensions—doesn't that equal fewer types of consequences for bad behavior?*

- *Fewer consequences for bad behavior equals less learning for all. Deterrents to bad behavior worked in the past, why not now?*

- *They endanger themselves, faculty, or classmates and/or prevent other students from learning.*

- *A principal needs to set standards and expectations for everyone to follow.*

(Continued)

(Continued)

- *I'm curious what the parental responsibility is. We continue to add society issues to the classroom/school without taking things off the classroom/school responsibilities list. Schools cannot be the total responsibility of fixing America's problems.*
- *At our school, students get suspended in cases where their behavior puts others in danger and we don't have the resources to deal with it. The few days gives the school time to put together a plan to deal with it. I think suspension has its place, but it should be a last resort.*
- *Maybe suspensions are issued so that parents assume the responsibility for behavior whereas teaching a student to read is the school's responsibility.*
- *Suspensions send a wake-up call to the parents; behavior is one thing that should be instilled by the parents.*
- *I was hired and trained to teach reading. When did it become the teachers' job to teach kids how to behave? Where are the parents?*

Did you feel any dissonance as you were going through this exercise? It is completely natural if you did. Typically, suspendable behaviors provoke strong emotional responses. There is a certain sense of security in using the traditional school discipline practices that have been in place for decades. Abraham Maslow has a quote we use to capture this phenomenon: "If the only tool you have is a hammer, you tend to see every problem as a nail." Not surprisingly, this quote is derived from Maslow's *Law of the Hammer*, which is a cognitive bias that involves an over-reliance on a familiar tool. We tend to simplify our responses to behavior by convincing ourselves suspensions (exclusionary practices) will change a student's behavior and keep other students physically and emotionally safe, when in fact it is a temporary fix to a more complex need and response. How would we, as adults, respond on our campus if our authoritative figures (administrators) used a traditional disciplinarian mindset (the hammer) for us in the workplace.

Rule:	Response:
Your contractual duty day begins at 7:30 a.m.	Gates will be locked at 7:31
The grading period ends Wednesday; your grades are due Thursday	You will be written up for not having them to me by Thursday at 3:00 p.m.
You questioned me in a staff meeting in front of the other teachers	Get out of my staff meeting. I need to set an example to show the other teachers this behavior is not tolerated.

We are fairly confident this response would at worst lead to a mutiny on a campus and at best erode the relationships and culture between staff and administration. We expect grace as adults, but do we give grace to students who are learning how to navigate through life using prosocial behaviors?

How Do We Become Innovators of This Work?

In order to change/shift thinking about alternative discipline, it is important to understand the various mindset shifts that need to occur. Figure 2.1 illustrates the natural distribution of a staff response to any new change idea.

Figure 2.1   Characteristics: Innovators to Laggards

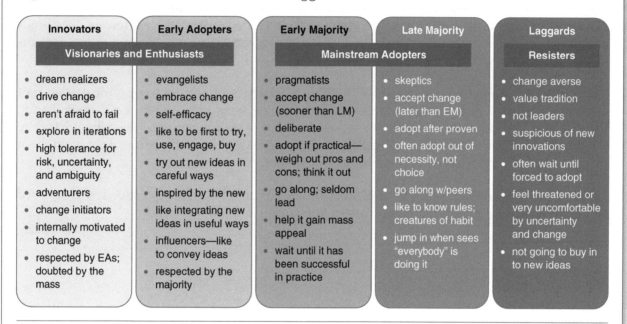

Innovators	Early Adopters	Early Majority	Late Majority	Laggards
Visionaries and Enthusiasts		**Mainstream Adopters**		**Resisters**
• dream realizers • drive change • aren't afraid to fail • explore in iterations • high tolerance for risk, uncertainty, and ambiguity • adventurers • change initiators • internally motivated to change • respected by EAs; doubted by the mass	• evangelists • embrace change • self-efficacy • like to be first to try, use, engage, buy • try out new ideas in careful ways • inspired by the new • like integrating new ideas in useful ways • influencers—like to convey ideas • respected by the majority	• pragmatists • accept change (sooner than LM) • deliberate • adopt if practical—weigh out pros and cons; think it out • go along; seldom lead • help it gain mass appeal • wait until it has been successful in practice	• skeptics • accept change (later than EM) • adopt after proven • often adopt out of necessity, not choice • go along w/peers • like to know rules; creatures of habit • jump in when sees "everybody" is doing it	• change averse • value tradition • not leaders • suspicious of new innovations • often wait until forced to adopt • feel threatened or very uncomfortable by uncertainty and change • not going to buy in to new ideas

Source: Reproduced with permission from The Center for Creative Emergence, 2019. Original main sources: *Diffusion of Innovation* by Everett Rogers; *Crossing the Chasm* by Geoffrey Moore.

There will be a range of opinions and reactions regarding your decision to use alternatives to suspension. Some staff will champion this work because they know it is best for students; some will be skeptical and will want to see that it works before fully supporting it; and others will flat out oppose and share their disapproval in the staff room to anyone who will listen. It makes no difference what state or province you are in or if you are at an elementary school, a middle school, or a high school; we can guarantee that you will have this range of reactions to this work. Understanding the characteristics in each level (Figure 2.1), you can position your response to provide staff with what they need to move from their current state to a more supportive position. Knowing this natural distribution will help you lead this work on your campus.

Here are our top three ways to shift mindsets and build ownership around alternative discipline:

1. BELIEVE IN WHAT YOU ARE DOING and OTHERS WILL FOLLOW

2. TRUST IN THE PROCESS OF ALTERNATIVE DISCIPLINE and OTHERS WILL FOLLOW

3. SHARE EVIDENCE OF SUCCESS and OTHERS WILL FOLLOW

(Continued)

(Continued)

First, *you* need to believe in this work. You need to be able to articulate your *why* and that the intentional teaching of behavior is more impactful than suspension. This is why it is so important your beliefs are in a place where you are carrying conviction to others, not just yourself.

Second, you'll need to trust that this is a process for supporting students. This is actually more time-consuming at first, but the investment of alternative discipline will pay off in the long run. The more time and effort put into teaching students prosocial behaviors, establishing relationships and trust, the less you are going to see repeated suspendable offenses. This is not a reaction to a new state metric or some new fad; it is a consistent process that is best for students. You have to trust the process so others will.

Third, the late adopters will need to see that this works. It is important to provide evidence of success. In other words, celebrate alternative discipline wins rather than focus on setbacks. One way to introduce this is by inviting a student into a staff meeting to describe what they learned through their alternative discipline consequences and how this process changed them (especially if it's a student who has a history of suspensions).

In the next chapter, we provide additional most commonly asked questions and tips for implementation no matter where you are in your implementation journey.

3

Questions and Tips Before You Begin

Everything used in this toolkit is based on needs from educators we work with. This book is written by practitioners for practitioners. These aren't theories or suggestions based on what we think may work. Here are the most commonly asked questions and tips before you begin.

IS ALTERNATIVE DISCIPLINE A ONE-SIZE-FITS-ALL APPROACH?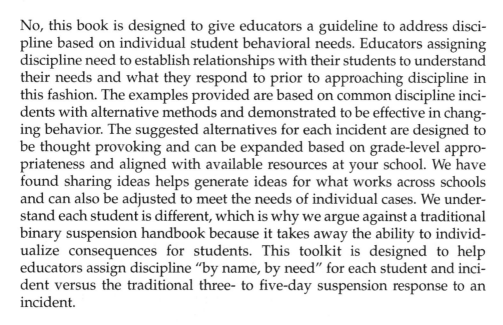

No, this book is designed to give educators a guideline to address discipline based on individual student behavioral needs. Educators assigning discipline need to establish relationships with their students to understand their needs and what they respond to prior to approaching discipline in this fashion. The examples provided are based on common discipline incidents with alternative methods and demonstrated to be effective in changing behavior. The suggested alternatives for each incident are designed to be thought provoking and can be expanded based on grade-level appropriateness and aligned with available resources at your school. We have found sharing ideas helps generate ideas for what works across schools and can also be adjusted to meet the needs of individual cases. We understand each student is different, which is why we argue against a traditional binary suspension handbook because it takes away the ability to individualize consequences for students. This toolkit is designed to help educators assign discipline "by name, by need" for each student and incident versus the traditional three- to five-day suspension response to an incident.

ARE CONVERSATIONS ABOUT USING ALTERNATIVE DISCIPLINE DIFFICULT TO HAVE?

Yes, communicating alternative discipline effectively can be a laborious task for administrators. Prior to giving an alternative to a student, the beliefs of the administrator must support it. If the administrator cannot articulate the significance of why the alternative is important, no other adult on that campus will believe it to be important. There is an art to assigning alternative discipline while working with the stakeholders (parents, teachers, students) and deciding consequences that are appropriate for a student that will change behavior. We want to be clear: The message isn't to simply *not* suspend. The message is this student is returning to your school regardless, so what are you doing to teach and ensure these behaviors are not repeating on your campus? Trust us—students would prefer to go home for a few days than deal with alternative consequences. When approaching discipline in this way, one of the most common questions you will hear is, "why didn't you just suspend this student?" Here are some strategies that will help guide difficult conversations around alternative forms of discipline:

Listen to the Stakeholders. Allow the stakeholders to vent and hear them out so you can rationalize what they are saying. They've just experienced the behavior that led to the referral and aren't in a place to listen to an alternative. Allow them to cool down so you can talk them through. Provide them with a safe opportunity to honestly share what they feel. If you do not do this, they will not buy in and the conversation will continue in the staff lounge without you.

Communicate in a Timely Manner. When a teacher sends a student to the office on a referral, they are expecting the behavior to be addressed and a consequence handed out. If the teacher sees the student return to class shortly thereafter, their impression of the outcome will be that the administrator simply said, "don't do that again, now go back to class." A teacher who is not communicated with will feel the incident was dismissed and not handled. It is essential to make it an expectation for yourself to communicate the consequence in a timely manner (same day).

Involve the Teacher in the Alternative and Use It to Teach. When time permits, involve the teacher in creating consequences. It will empower the teacher as an authoritarian in the eyes of the student and someone who levies consequences. It will also bolster the teacher's beliefs around using discipline as a means to teach behavior. Additionally, it will allow them to see how much time and effort goes into doing discipline in this fashion. If they are given the opportunity to be included in the process, it will increase buy-in and support from the teacher.

Liken Behavior to Academics—Behavior RTI/Academic RTI. It is important to articulate the relationship between how adults respond to students who struggle to learn with how they respond to students who struggle to behave. When stakeholders hear the rationale behind why teaching academics is similar to teaching behavior, they are more willing to shift their thinking about how the discipline should be handled. A student struggling to read is not sent home for a few days and expected to return reading; likewise, a student struggling to behave needs more support to change behavior rather than suspension.

Question Beliefs. Be prepared for tough conversations about discipline and beliefs. It is important to get to the core beliefs of the teacher in order to help them work through and support an effective alternative consequence. One helpful method to peel the layers and get to the root/function of the problem behavior and possible solutions is the "five whys" approach or sequential questioning. For example:

Why do you want this student suspended from your class? He is being defiant.

Why is he being defiant? Because I told him to stop talking and complete his assignment and he didn't.

How did calmly giving him directions trigger the defiance? I yelled it out in front of the class because I was frustrated.

Why have you not asked for help with this student? I didn't want it to seem like I don't know how to handle my class.

Why do you think suspending him from your class today is going to change his behavior when he comes back tomorrow? I don't. I needed to make a point and show him who's boss.

Do you think you made your point? No, actually, I don't. I just needed a break.

Let's work together on a long-term consequence/intervention so you do not have to continue feeling this way.

If we are not forced to question our beliefs about discipline, we cannot get to the level of accepting alternative discipline in place of traditional methods.

HOW CAN WE APPROACH DISCIPLINE IN THIS WAY IF WE DO NOT HAVE THE BUDGET, RESOURCES, OR PERSONNEL FOR IT?

We realize not all schools have the same level of support staff or human capital available to them. We've seen schools make this work without a school psychologist or counselor; a two- or five-day-a-week school psychologist and/or counselor; an assistant principal; or none of the above and only a site principal. Ultimately, a school's response to discipline rests with those who make the decision whether a student goes home on a suspension or stays on campus. If suspension is your answer, is the student returning to your campus when the suspension ends? If so, what are you doing to prevent the behavior from repeating? We would argue simply using a reactive approach to discipline pulls more time and resources away from a site than a preventive approach. Furthermore, state and federal policies are being continually updated to include more support for social-emotional learning that aligns with this framework for alternative discipline. If a school wants to make preventive discipline work, a goal can be written into their school site plan to allocate funding to support initiatives that decrease suspensions and improve school culture. However, not having the budget, resources, or personnel is a common rationale used by some administrators to absolve themselves from any responsibility to support students who struggle behaviorally. If they invest in creating a schoolwide behavior system (RTI behavior) with a focus on prevention, they will see a decrease in the number of major incidents that occur at their school requiring the use of alternative discipline.

DO THE PROVIDED ALTERNATIVE DISCIPLINE EXAMPLES PERTAIN TO ALL GRADE LEVELS?

Yes, the examples provided are based on real-life alternative discipline examples from elementary, secondary, and alternative education settings. As the educator, you can take the suggested alternatives in this book and differentiate them for the specific grade levels on your campus. For example, two third-grade students fighting during a soccer game at recess in an elementary school is different than two high school students fighting in the quad during lunch; however, the suggested alternatives to restore and reteach appropriate behaviors will work for both. We've heard high school staff say, "that tool won't work for us, it's for elementary ages" and elementary staff say, "that tool won't work for us, that's for high school students." *For the same tool!* Remember, it's the thinking behind the tool that we want you to experience. The outcome is to teach and change behavior, not to universally apply a one-size-fits-all approach. These tools can be applied to any grade level, but they are also intended to change your thinking from punishment to discipline.

IS IT HARDER TO APPROACH DISCIPLINE IN THIS WAY?

Yes, using alternatives is a more difficult way of responding to discipline. It requires individualized attention to the student(s) that is fundamentally different than being sent home for a few days and expecting them to return behaving. Alternatives use discipline to teach behavior similar to how we teach academics. Using alternatives can be challenging. Expect to be questioned by stakeholders (parents, teachers, district leadership, etc.) who expect a traditional approach to discipline. Communication is essential; obviously due to student confidentiality, you cannot communicate a student's consequences to any parent other than their own. However, it is necessary to let the teacher know what you plan to use as an alternative to get buy-in and involve them in the process. We would also recommend including your district's supervisor of Child Welfare and Attendance or area administrator from the district when using alternatives for more serious infractions. Some districts still have zero-tolerance board policies and outdated handbooks that are years behind current state and federal policy recommendations and/or a belief system built around supporting students when it comes to behavior. As an administrator in a position where board policy is at a rigid dichotomy with using alternative means of correction for discipline, you will want to explain the incident and how you intend to handle it with your direct supervisor to gain support until policies are updated to include the use of alternatives.

DOES THE LANGUAGE IN YOUR SCHOOL/DISTRICT HANDBOOK OR BOARD POLICIES SUPPORT THE USE OF ALTERNATIVE DISCIPLINE?

For this work to be aligned across a district and to prevent an administrator from feeling isolated against their own district policies, it is important that the language in the school or district discipline handbook is updated and aligned to support the use of an alternative discipline approach. Here is an example of a brief addition to handbook language supportive of alternative discipline practices:

Sample Language: The district supports the school administrator's use of other means of correction for suspendable offenses, specifically alternative discipline restorative practices in lieu of suspension.

IS THIS WORK HARDER IF YOU DO NOT HAVE THE ALIGNMENT WITH THE DISTRICT OFFICE AND SCHOOL BOARD?

Here are the key differences we have found between *supportive* and *unsupportive* district office practices when it comes to implementing alternative discipline in lieu of suspensions in schools:

Supportive—(clarity)	vs.	Unsupportive—(confusion)
Clear and consistent district-wide initiatives		Too many initiatives
Training and supports in place to build the capacity of the administrators and school staff on initiatives aligned with clear goals and outcomes		Inadequate training and supports; inconsistency of initiatives

(Continued)

(Continued)

Supportive—(clarity)	vs.	Unsupportive—(confusion)
Updated policies in regard to discipline with intentional language that allows for alternative discipline and restorative practices		Policies not updated to match the changes in state and federal policy recommendations
Working with school administration on discipline decisions that require collaboration between the school and district due to the sensitivity or the severity of the discipline		Reversing administrator decisions about alternative discipline due to external/political pressures
Educates the school board and community on the importance of addressing discipline similar to academics; allows opportunities for the community and school board to address their concerns and needs in regard to such topics		Inability to articulate and defend the purpose of alternative discipline to the school board or community

If district mission or vision statements continue to claim they address the needs of *all* students, it may be time to revisit practices, policies, and procedures that support such statements. A mission or vision statement is just words on a webpage unless the actions at all levels, from the board-room to the classroom, support and bring it to life. Educators often speak about the importance of creating a positive school culture, yet we forget about the ripple effects an unsupportive district office culture has on schools. We challenge site and district office administration to evaluate their current discipline practices and reflect on the student groups who are disproportionately impacted by such practices. Are these practices aligned to our mission/vision and commitments around the way we support *all* students across our district? Consider these two short excerpts from emails from a supportive and unsupportive superintendent.

Superintendent A:

Dear Educators,

We have worked hard together to create a culture of restorative practices in our schools. I know this is not easy work, but we know it is worth the effort. We are committed to a culture of helping every child, even those who make poor decisions to learn and grow from their mistakes. I encourage you to continue changing the narrative on inequities in school discipline at your schools. Remember, the decisions you make will change the trajectory of the future of so many of our students and communities.

Superintendent B:

Dear Educators,

As you have noticed, there has been a rise in aggressive behaviors in our schools. We will not tolerate this behavior. Please make sure to review our zero-tolerance policies and share them with parents as well. All students who do not follow the behaviors listed on the policy will receive an automatic five-day suspension.

WHEN DO WE USE ALTERNATIVE DISCIPLINE?

Use alternative discipline any time you want to teach and change behavior and for incidents where a student would return to your school from a suspension. We understand there are times when students will be placed into an alternative setting or other more serious consequences for their behavior. However, even when a student is placed in an alternative setting and will not return to your campus, we suggest that the alternative discipline still take place as part of the transition into their new placement. Moving the problem behavior does not resolve the fact that the student still needs the opportunity to learn from the decisions they have made that placed them in their new alternative setting. Remember, the goal is to produce productive members in our community, not shift a behavior problem from one campus to another.

WHY IS IT IMPORTANT TO DEVELOP AND MONITOR SCHOOL SUSPENSION SMART GOALS?

Developing and monitoring school-wide and student subgroup suspension SMART (Strategic and Specific, Measurable, Attainable/Achievable, Results Oriented, and Time-Bound) goals is also critical for addressing inequities and disproportionality in school discipline for underserved student populations. It is important for the site administration to shine a light on this disproportionality, have ongoing difficult conversations about these statistics, and work to change the narrative. Here is an example of a school's (school-wide and students with disabilities subgroup) SMART goals monitored at least monthly by the site's behavior team using the form on the next page.

Sample school-wide SMART goal: By the end of the 2022–2023 school year, the total number of unduplicated suspensions at XXX School will decrease at least 50% school-wide when compared to 2021–2022 suspension data. Note: Baseline data for 2021–2022 is 30 unduplicated suspensions. Goal will be 15 or fewer for 2022–2023.

Sample Suspension SMART Goal Monitoring Tool:

School-wide Suspension SMART Goal	Aug	Sept	Oct	Nov	Dec	Jan	Feb	March	April	May	June
By the end of the 2022–2023 school year, the total number of unduplicated suspensions at XXX School will decrease at least 50% school-wide when compared to 2021–2022 suspension data. Note: Baseline data for 2021–2022 is 30 unduplicated suspensions. Goal will be 15 or fewer for 2022–2023.											

Students Receiving Special Education Services Subgroup SMART Goal	Aug	Sept	Oct	Nov	Dec	Jan	Feb	March	April	May	June
By the end of the 2022–2023 school year, the total number of unduplicated suspensions for students with disabilities at XXX School will decrease at least 50% when compared to 2021–2022 suspension data. Note: Baseline data for 2021–2022 is 14 unduplicated suspensions. Goal will be 7 or fewer for 2022–2023.											

Sample students with disabilities SMART goal: By the end of the 2022–2023 school year, the total number of unduplicated suspensions for students with disabilities at XXX School will decrease at least 50% when compared to 2021–2022 suspension data. Note: Baseline data for 2021–2022 is 14 unduplicated suspensions. Goal will be 7 or fewer for 2022–2023.

WHEN DO SCHOOLS PROVIDE ALTERNATIVE DISCIPLINE, AND WHO PROVIDES IT?

It depends. With respect to *who*, the design of the alternative discipline contract should be a collaborative effort with key stakeholders. With that said, working together as a collaborative alternative discipline team, it is important to assign different responsibilities among staff depending on those directly impacted by the student's behavior, those with training and skills to support this student (i.e., counselor, school psychologist, or social worker), an adult to serve as a mentor (i.e., a coach or teacher), and of course the administrator to communicate this network of support that is being created for this student and to monitor the contract. The point is this work does not land on one person to ensure the alternative discipline is taking place as designed. For example, in the event of vandalism, one possible collaborative response could consist of an administrator, custodian, and school counselor (the counselor takes the lead on the instructional and reflective component of teaching appropriate behavior, the custodian monitors the restitution component, and the administrator monitors the student's progress on the remaining components of the contract). This is just one example of many variations a school could choose as a possible response to support this student. With respect to *when*, we have seen schools provide alternative discipline during a carved-out block of time with a credentialed educator prior to school, during loss of privileges, after school, and Saturday school.

IS IT DIFFICULT TO ACHIEVE TEACHER OWNERSHIP OF THIS ALTERNATIVE DISCIPLINE APPROACH?

Yes, you will most certainly have a difficult time achieving ownership from teachers if you do not educate teachers on what alternative discipline is, if teachers do not feel they have a voice, if they do not feel supported, and if you do not follow through on a student's alternative discipline contract.

It does not matter what state we travel to and listen to educators' personal experiences firsthand—there is a consistent and definite disconnect between a referral and the communication of consequences from their administrator. The best way to achieve ownership from teachers is through effective communication *and* involving them in the alternative discipline process. Allow for teacher voice and for them to be a collaborative partner in this work. This will also strengthen the relationship between the student and teacher. Remember, the focus is to teach through consequences rather than punishment through exclusion.

HOW IS ALTERNATIVE DISCIPLINE CONNECTED TO SOCIAL AND EMOTIONAL LEARNING (SEL) SKILLS?

As educators, we do a great job identifying the absence of specific academic skills impeding a student's ability to succeed in a particular content area—for example, a non-fluent reader needing additional support with vowel blends and digraphs or a student not able to recall basic math facts, procedures, rules, or formulas hindering their success in math. However, when it comes to behaviors, we suddenly attach labels, such as acting out, being disruptive, or being lazy. Why is it that our focus shifts from a student demonstrating gaps in learning based on the absence of a specific skill, identifying those skills, and providing support by teaching these skills to get that student back on track with reading or math, yet when we identify students demonstrating specific behaviors, we don't view it as a student requiring the necessary instruction needed to learn a specific SEL skill so they reduce or eliminate those undesirable behaviors? We respect and appreciate the comprehensive definition and science of SEL from CASEL.org that has been derived from extensive research in this area.

CASEL.org defines SEL

> as a process through which all young people and adults acquire and apply knowledge, skills, and attitudes to develop healthy identities, manage emotions and achieve personal and collective goals, feel and show empathy for others, establish and maintain supportive relationships, and make responsible and caring decisions. The CASEL 5 are the five areas highlighted: self-awareness, self-management, social awareness, relationship skills, and responsible decision-making.

If you are implementing alternative discipline correctly by assigning restorative, reflective, and instructional components, you will in fact be teaching essential SEL skills too! Our book *SEL From a Distance* can also be used as a complementary resource to provide additional ways to teach SEL skills as part of alternative discipline. Below you will see how each component from our alternative discipline framework aligns to each of the five SEL competencies.

Alternative Discipline Framework	What SEL skills are these components helping to address?
Restorative (to repair relationships harmed)	Relationship skills
Reflective (to understand how your behavior has impacted you and others)	Self-awareness Social awareness
Instructional (to learn new skills to not engage in the behavior again)	Self-management Responsible decision-making

WHAT IF THE PARENT SAYS "NO" TO THE ALTERNATIVE DISCIPLINE?

First, let's view this experience through a parent's lens. The school administrator calls you at work to inform you that your child just committed a suspendable offense. As a parent, I'm wanting to know every detail of the incident and if my baby will be treated fairly. If another student was involved, I want to know that they will receive the same "severity" of consequences as my child.

Here is where the power of relationships comes in. If I have a student who is repeatedly on the school's radar for misbehavior, I need to make sure that for every negative phone call home or interaction that I am creating at least four positive experiences with that family. Think of it as emotional currency—every negative experience is a withdrawal and every positive experience is a deposit. If all the family experiences are withdrawals from their emotional "bank account" with the school, that emotional account will be quickly overdrawn. Then, when I need support from this family, my account will say "insufficient funds" and they will resist nearly any request I make because they will view me as picking on their child. However, when that emotional account is filled and I need to make a "withdrawal," they will be more likely to support my decisions because I've got their child's back since I've created many more positive experiences than negative.

Frame this conversation I'm about to model below through this simple scientific fact: *A human brain is developing from the time of conception until approximately age 25.*

We know that students will make mistakes in life. When they do, we will be there to *support* them so they learn from their mistakes and don't engage in these behaviors again.

A parent's reaction to this information is largely shaped by how we deliver its message. Now, when that phone call comes and I say "hi, Mrs. Jones, this is John, principal at Washington. Sorry to interrupt you at work; I'm calling because Bobby just did _____, which is a three- to five-day suspendable offense" (I pause for a few seconds to let that register how a suspension will impact their work schedule or childcare plans); then I say, "however, at Washington we believe that when students make mistakes, we need to provide opportunities for them to learn from those mistakes to prevent them from repeating. With that being said, rather than suspending Bobby from school, I will be supporting him during the school day through a series of _____" (list some of the restorative, reflective, and instructional opportunities Bobby will receive). "He will remain in the learning environment so he can stay current on all of his instructional content, but he will lose privileges while completing these tasks to earn all of his privileges back."

Mrs. Jones: "No, Bobby won't be taking part in any of those things. Send him home on a suspension."

"Mrs. Jones, it is our responsibility as a school to provide Bobby with the skills so that he doesn't engage in these behaviors again. We, as a school, also have an obligation to the families that we serve to provide a safe school environment free from disruptive behaviors. This path is showing grace and compassion because we care so much for Bobby's future and well-being. If we didn't care about your son, we would simply send him home for three to five days and dismiss these actions. These alternatives that we are choosing in lieu of suspension will take much more time and resources from myself and our staff to *support* your son because we care so much about his success at our school and for his future. The easiest response from this school would be to remove him from our campus, but that is not what is best for Bobby; I hope you understand."

Nine out of 10 parents at this point would be gracious of the school's position, but there is that .01% who may still say, "I don't care, send him home."

At which point, my response is, "This call was to inform you of the actions your child engaged in and to communicate the school's response to prevent these actions from further taking place on our campus. I want you to know that we care about Bobby's success as much as you do, which is why we are providing the support so he doesn't engage in these behaviors again. Thank you for your understanding." This last response indicates this call was communication from the school, not permission seeking. It also communicates that the school is still choosing to put Bobby's needs first.

The key to this conversation is that we are using this experience to *teach* rather than *punish* Bobby. Any reasonable parent who sees the school making every effort to use an opportunity where their child made a significant mistake to support and give corrective opportunities as to not re-engage in these behaviors again will be very gracious and supportive of these efforts. If they view it as a punishment, they will hunker down and protect their child, because as parents they reserve the right to be the sole authority to punish their child.

 ## WHAT IF THE STUDENT SAYS "NO" TO THE ALTERNATIVE DISCIPLINE?

Let's first take an empathetic approach and experience this through the student's lens. They have just engaged in some form of disruptive, defiant, or troublesome misbehavior and will be in a heightened state of arousal and feeling a wide range of emotions. This isn't the time to use an aggressive interrogative approach of "what were you thinking?!," which will ultimately result in the student lashing out further or shutting down. This is the time to make every effort to connect with the student, check that they are okay and that factors in their life (outside of school) are okay. This is the time to let them know that they are in a safe place and surrounded by adults who care. Yes, they made a mistake/poor decision (and there will be consequences), but now is the time to get them to a regulated state so we can process through these consequences together. The only way to get them there is for them to have the emotional safety from the adults in the room.

Begin explaining that there are consequences for behaviors in life: "If I run a red light or get a ticket for speeding, I will need to pay a fine, go to traffic school, and potentially have it affect my driving record and pay higher insurance rates—these are consequences for choices I've made. As a student, there are consequences for the choices you make. As a school, it is our job to prepare you for a life outside of school. We are preparing you to also be a productive member of our community. In addition to teaching you academic content, we are also here to support you when you make decisions that can negatively impact your future as an adult. As a school, it is also our job to create a safe school environment that is free from disruptive behaviors so all students can learn and thrive. The same way we cannot have a society where there are no consequences for running red lights, the same applies to our school. With that said, since you engaged in _____, this is the alternative discipline contract that we will use for the next five days to learn from this experience. This infraction would carry a three- to five-day suspension, but sending you home for three to five days is the easy thing to do. Because I care about you and I know you are a good person, I can't allow you to engage in these behaviors again. Which is why I'm willing to put the time in to support you in completing this alternative discipline contract. This is going to take a considerable amount of my and my staff's time. If I didn't care about you, I would send you home on a suspension. Remember, it is my job to prepare you to be a productive member of our community and for life. So, starting tomorrow _____" (and list the plan moving forward).

In my experiences, this approach has created students who (1) are surprised an adult is willing to put extra time into supporting them and not using the traditional approach of suspension they've experienced in the past; (2) are shocked their behavior is being met with compassion and grace rather than the usual animosity and vexation that adults may have previously treated them with; and (3) continue to follow me around campus or go out of their way to see me even after the completion of their alternative discipline contract, because they were so desperate to feel connected to something at school.

This approach will create an experience where a student knows there are consequences for behavior. It flips their experience into choices; you choose to engage in these negative behaviors, you choose the consequences that are connected to them. You don't engage in these behaviors, you'll enjoy all the privileges that are awarded to all students demonstrating appropriate behavior. It shifts from a defensive position of "you're picking on me" to "I've made this poor choice and these are the consequences I've chosen as a result."

Nine out of 10 students at this point would accept their alternative discipline consequences. However, there are times when a student will say, "No." There are a variety of options to take at this point:

1. Provide a visual—Give the student a calendar with each day filled in for their alternative consequences so they can see their start and end point. This gives them a visual showing for each day they refuse the consequences keep getting bumped further across the calendar. Remember, the student has lost all privileges during this time so a five-day consequence with three days of refusal results in eight days of zero privileges and now zero days of consequences met. The calendar allows them to see what would have been a Monday start day and Friday finish is now a student on Thursday still waiting to start day 1 and their refusal is now leading to their consequences moving into the following week.

2. Differentiate—Is it a won't do or a can't do? If it's a won't do, see item #1 above. If it's a can't do because the alternative consequence involves researching and writing a reflection but the student lacks the reading or writing skills necessary to complete this task, differentiate it for them. Allow them to watch a video and give a verbal reflection to the administrator. For younger students, have them draw a picture and the administrator can transcribe what they are saying so you have a record of their thoughts.

3. Choice—Often students will refuse because they feel a loss of control, and through refusal they feel they have control over the situation. When we give students choice (i.e., write a reflection *or* project-based learning), it gives them a sense of control *and* either choice still results in a win-win toward the completion of their contract.

4. Rally for more support—Identify a person in the child's life whom that student trusts. For example, we have worked with a coach, karate instructor, and grandfather to help the student trust the process.

5. Be relentless—Behavior is a form of communication. This student needs to know the adults are not going to give up on them. Students can see the adults who are authentic and believe in them and the ones who do not.

💼 AUTHORS' NOTE

We know this chapter is titled "Questions and Tips Before You Begin," but the lessons learned and tips embedded in each response are useful for wherever you are in this journey. Put a sticky note to mark this section because you will revisit it as you hear these aforementioned questions and will use these tips as these situations arise. We guarantee it!

4

Alternative Discipline

As school administrators, we have both experienced the emotions and challenges connected with students making poor decisions that result in school discipline/consequences. We have also experienced the pushback from teachers, parents, and district leadership that comes with not following a black-and-white handbook approach to discipline (*Cautionary note: We are not saying a district should not have general disciplinary guidelines to follow; we are saying the handbook should be updated to include a comprehensive response to student behavior, rather than a one-size-fits-all approach*). This requires thinking beyond the traditional method of sending students home and hoping that their parents will teach them not to do it again or being home from school will teach them not to do it again. It also requires that the message to students, teachers, and parents isn't "we just don't suspend anymore." Opponents to alternatives argue the message sent to students who misbehave is that there are no consequences for their actions because they know they won't be suspended. We would argue, if that is the culture of your school, you aren't using alternatives effectively. When used correctly, the alternative will be much more impactful and meaningful than simply sending a student home for a few days. When a school has effective systematic tiers of behavioral supports in place and utilizes effective alternatives that are restorative, reflective, and instructional, you will see a dramatic reduction in the number of incidents and a significant increase in the positive culture on your campus. Innovative discipline teaches students real-life lessons and the impact their behavior has on others, the community, and their future. We have an obligation to help students become productive members of the community by preparing them academically as well as social-emotionally to succeed.

WHAT IS ALTERNATIVE DISCIPLINE?

Alternative discipline is a framework for assigning meaningful discipline to students. Alternative discipline has to include a restorative, reflective, and instructional component. Administrators can use any combination of the three (two restorative, two instructional, and one reflective); there isn't a secret formula for how many of each to use as long as you include all three. This framework is centered around two questions: (1) Is this a discipline incident that is resulting in the student returning back to my campus? If yes, an innovative disciplinarian will use an alternative form of discipline, rather than simply sending the student home on a suspension; and (2) Does the consequence have real-life application and meaning to help improve student behavior? The consequence needs to be meaningful for the student and privileges need to be earned back based on completion of the alternative discipline contract. The only way it will be meaningful is if the administrator or educator listens to the student to learn the function of the behavior and establishes a relationship with the student throughout the alternative discipline process.

For the purpose of this book, we define restorative, reflective, and instructional as follows:

Restorative: Provides opportunities for the student to restore relationships between themselves and stakeholder(s) they have affected due to the behavior incident (apology, student contracts, community service, restitution, etc.).

Reflective: Provides opportunities for students to reflect about the decisions they made that led to the discipline (reflection sheets, role-playing, scenarios, interviews, etc.).

Instructional: Provides teaching opportunities for students that target the function of the behavior and helps them learn the skills needed to not engage in such behaviors again (behavior lessons, social skills, teaching opportunities, behavior exams, etc.).

Discipline must be viewed as an opportunity to teach and change behavior. Consequences must be strategically planned and intentionally implemented based on each student by name, by need the same way a school system responds to a student who struggles to learn academically. As you can imagine, this approach is much more time-consuming for an administrator; however, seeing a student's behavior change because you believed in them is equally as fulfilling as seeing a student learn because a teacher believed in and supported them. We have added the Don't Suspend Me Readiness Checklist to help you assess your readiness for implementation.

We created a short checklist to help educators prepare for effective implementation. We wish we had this checklist as a reference when we began implementation as site administrators.

Don't Suspend Me Readiness Checklist

Check all that apply.

Leadership	☐ Are those leading the alternative discipline implementation demonstrating ownership of it? ☐ Is the vision for alternative discipline clearly defined? ☐ Is the school's discipline handbook updated to support the use of alternative discipline (restorative) practices? ☐ Is the district office leadership on board with alternative discipline implementation? ☐ Is the school board aware of alternative discipline practices?
People (Stakeholders)	☐ Are the benefits of implementing alternative discipline clear to all stakeholders? ☐ Are there plans in place to provide ongoing training for all stakeholders? ☐ Have families been educated on alternative discipline practices?
Communication	☐ Is a communication structure in place for working with all stakeholders on alternative discipline implementation? ☐ Are there check-ins set up for ongoing feedback from all stakeholders on how alternative discipline is going? ☐ What is our process for communicating alternative discipline needs to all stakeholders?
Culture	☐ Has the context around current discipline practices been assessed? ☐ Has feedback about discipline been collected from stakeholders? ☐ Is it made clear how the alternative discipline work is connected to the school's mission and goals?
Process	☐ Is the plan for implementing alternative discipline clearly defined? ☐ Is there an ongoing training plan established? ☐ Do we collect and monitor student suspension data (i.e., SMART goals) on a regular basis? ☐ Do we have accountability structures built in to ensure effective implementation?

In Part II, you will find case study examples of how to assign alternative discipline. Part III provides a menu of alternative discipline options for the most common behavior incidents in schools that result in suspensions. Part IV will help you organize what you have learned and bring it all together.

PART II

Case Studies on
Alternative Discipline

5

Case Studies

In this chapter, you will find five case study examples of alternative discipline in action. This will allow you to see how the menu of alternative discipline suggestions can be translated through these specific case studies. It is important to understand that conducting alternative discipline requires more time and resources, therefore, it is critical to first create an effective tiered behavior system at your school so fewer students will engage in behaviors that result in this type of discipline. Taking the time to invest in this type of discipline will decrease the chances of the behaviors reoccurring.

You will also notice the alternative discipline in the highlighted case studies include at least one restorative, one reflective, and one instructional example in the assigned discipline and organized into components. As you read these case studies, imagine your school setting and resources that would allow you to address discipline in this way.

Ask yourself the following reflective questions as you read each case study:

1. Does the assigned alternative discipline seem effective?

2. Would you consider assigning discipline in this way?

3. What steps do you need to take to create a culture at your school to discipline in this way?

4. Do you think this type of discipline is more valuable than sending students home?

5. What will be your first step in implementing discipline in this way?

ALTERNATIVE DISCIPLINE
CASE STUDY 1: FIGHTING

During recess, two sixth-grade male students began arguing over the rules during a football game. This topic has been an ongoing debate between these two boys for the past several weeks. On this particular day, the students were yelling at each other during the game, which attracted a crowd. The yard duty teacher noticed the commotion and was able to intervene. She pulled the boys aside and had them apologize to each other and made them agree not to engage in such behavior again. Both boys agreed to follow the rules, but they were not over the conflict from the game. Although the yard duty teacher believed she had resolved the conflict, she did not realize that one of the students could not move past what he believed to be an injustice and had his friends tell the other boy to meet him in the bathroom after school to fight. The other boy did not want to meet him but was taunted by his peers to do so throughout the school day. After school, he reluctantly met in the bathroom and engaged in a fight to resolve the issue from the morning football game. The administrator got word of the fight and was able to intervene shortly after it started. After stopping the fight, the administrator had a choice to make about the consequence given. She knew both of these boys and had dealt with them through suspensions in the past, so she challenged herself to try something different knowing her other methods were not effective up to this point. She wanted to make sure the consequence was one that would teach the importance of handling conflict appropriately in the future. Traditionally, she would have referenced the school discipline handbook and suspended them both for three days but decided to look at this discipline differently.

Below is the response from the administrator that changed behavior for both students as well as how she approached discipline from this point forward. The handling of this incident was also a catalyst to how students and staff at her school viewed the commitment to changing behavior. In the past, she would have used the short conflict resolution script she was trained to use for incidents similar to this one, but she decided to take it several steps deeper into the conflict and resolution. Her steps were simple and to the point with the students. She brought the boys into her office and explained the phases of their consequence. After hearing them, one student actually said he would prefer to be suspended than have to complete all the alternative components of the consequence. He told the administrator he had been suspended plenty of times before and at least this way the consequence would be over when he came back to school. The administrator asked the student if being suspended helped change his behavior. The boy answered, "for a little bit, until someone else made me mad." So, she decided at this point to use alternative discipline that was designed to help change behavior for the long term.

Alternative Discipline

Restorative: Together, they began by completing a restorative behavior contract with each other. Each student had to share where they felt an injustice took place, write an apology to each other, commit to a resolution, and agree to the progress monitoring terms of the agreement they created together. Both students along with the administrator signed the document.

Instructional: They were assigned six sessions each of hands-off academy. Hands-off academy was designed to provide a behavior teaching opportunity for both students to learn other methods of resolving conflict rather than through violence. In these courses, the administrator taught coping strategies to the students when dealing with conflict and checked the application of learned skills through behavior scenarios and a culminating behavior exam.

Reflective: The students had a set check-in date and time with the administrator on a weekly basis where they had to progress monitor their restorative contract and learn about each other. They were asked to both derive 30 questions they wanted answered about each other, interview each other, and prepare a presentation about the other student. This allowed them to have a safe space to learn about the other and how to accept similarities and differences.

Instructional: Both boys were assigned a project aligned with sports game rules and character. They had to present the rules of the football game to the sixth-grade class and provide strategies for students to use when they become upset during a sports game. In addition, they had to serve as referees of football during lunch with an emphasis on identifying students following the rules and showing character.

Restorative: Both boys were celebrated for their hard work learning from this major behavior incident at their school. They both had to write a reflection about what they learned from this experience and create an individual contract ensuring they would not engage in this type of behavior again.

 ## ALTERNATIVE DISCIPLINE CASE STUDY 2: THEFT

A female middle school student noticed the vice principal dropped her cell phone during supervision. Instead of picking it up and giving it back to the administrator, she decided to keep it for herself. In her next two class periods, she bragged about stealing the cell phone while going through the pictures and text messages. An anonymous student reported what she heard in class to the administrator. The administrator was able to conduct an investigation that led to her retrieving her cell phone from the student. However, when she called the mother of the student to report what happened and explained she would be assigning traditional discipline (suspension), the mother told the administrator her daughter had not stolen the phone but in fact she had just purchased it for her. The administrator confirmed with the mother that this was her phone and it was stolen. This parent's defense of her child's theft confirmed that sending the student home on a suspension would not teach correct behavior, so the administrator provided an alternative, real-world consequence for theft.

Alternative Discipline

Restorative: The administrator met with the student and discussed why she stole the cell phone in the first place. The administrator walked the student through a restorative agreement contract, so it was clear how taking another person's property impacts others. Together, they developed an agreement and began their plan on moving forward to restore the injustice that had taken place.

Instructional: The student had to research the consequences of stealing in the community. She was assigned a five-paragraph essay that had to include evidence from at least four sources. The topic prompt she had to respond to was as follows: What are ways to earn trust back from a person(s) you have stolen from? What are consequences of this type of behavior in the community? What have you learned from this experience? The essay needed to be signed off by the administration and address all provided prompts.

Reflective: The student was assigned an apology letter to complete for the administrator and teacher of the classroom she had interrupted by bragging about the incident.

Restorative: The student was assigned a mentor on campus to provide support through weekly check-ins to ensure the student is on track. The student has input on who the mentor will be (an adult she respects). The student is assigned community service with a time span aligned with the cost of the stolen item and will be signed off by the mentor and administrator upon completion of hours.

Reflective: The student will create and sign a contract ensuring this behavior will never take place again in the school or community.

ALTERNATIVE DISCIPLINE
CASE STUDY 3: SEXUAL HARASSMENT

A high school male student showed inappropriate pictures to other students in class on his cell phone. He also made inappropriate sexual comments to female students in class and throughout campus. He specifically enjoyed making inappropriate comments to a female student he had a crush on and was not understanding that she did not like the attention he was giving her. It made her feel unsafe at school and anxious to be in class with him.

Alternative Discipline

Restorative: The administrator conducted a restorative agreement with the two students in a safe space. During this session, the female student was able to tell him how his actions made her feel, with the administrator facilitating. Together, they agreed on a contract to be monitored by the administrator on an ongoing basis.

Restorative: The male student was assigned to write apology letters to the female student, the teacher, and the parents of the female student. In addition, if consent is received, he will make a personal phone call to the parents of the female student or personally meet with them (with the administrator present) to make certain their daughter feels safe at school and these behaviors will end.

Reflective: The student will interview three important women in his life about how they would feel if someone showed them inappropriate pictures of women and constantly made sexual comments to them. He had to present his findings from the interviews to the administrator.

Instructional: The student will read the district handbook description on sexual harassment and identify a sexual harassment description in a work environment within the community. Specifically, he will have to research sexual harassment laws within the field of work he plans to be employed in the future. He will have to write an essay describing what he has learned from these descriptions. The essay will report what he has learned through this research and what the consequences would be for his career and within the community if he continued to engage in these types of behaviors as an adult.

Instructional: He had to participate in four sessions with a school counselor to role-play appropriate ways to respectfully seek peer attention from female students. In these sessions, he was provided scenarios and taught strategies to handle them appropriately.

Restorative: He had to meet with the female student in a safe place with the administrator present and share what he learned from this experience. He will also create an individual behavior contract identifying his commitment to changing his behavior.

ALTERNATIVE DISCIPLINE
CASE STUDY 4: BULLYING

> A bully doesn't stop being a bully because they were sent home
> for three days.

Two female ninth-grade students have been engaged in bullying of another female student online during and after school hours since the beginning of their eighth-grade school year. They have been suspended for these behaviors in the eighth grade but have continued the behavior into ninth grade. Most recently, these two students created an online social media account using the other female student's name and profile picture. With this account, they began posting inappropriate comments and pictures during school hours, resulting in much distress, torment, and worry for the female student. Fortunately, an upstander student reported what was happening to a trusted teacher and the teacher shared the information immediately with a school administrator.

An investigation revealed the feud had originally begun over a boyfriend and all three girls were best friends for years prior to this incident. In addition, a phone call to the past administration from the feeder middle school confirmed the two female students had been suspended in the past for this behavior and were directed to stay away from the other student upon their return to school from their suspensions. The administrator also met with the student being bullied and had a conversation with her. At first, the student was hesitant to share because she revealed what usually happens is the two female students stop calling her names or doing things online to hurt her temporarily, and then as soon as the teachers and administrators forget about the incident(s), they begin again. She shared this experience has changed her in so many ways. She said she is afraid to come to school, has difficulty making new friends, has a low self-concept, and does not feel like she can go to anyone for help. After collecting this information, the administrator begins developing an alternative discipline with all stakeholder input.

Alternative Discipline

Reflective: The two female students were interviewed individually and then together by the administrator to identify the root cause of the behaviors. Both students were asked to complete a student version of the alternative discipline contract to gather their input on what they believe is an appropriate consequence for their behaviors.

Restorative: The two female students were asked to identify those on their list in the student version of the alternative discipline contract to begin the restorative process, beginning with the student they were bullying. Individually, the students were asked to apologize to the other student in a safe space utilizing the restorative contract process with an administrator or administrator designee. In addition to the contracts developed, a check-in mentor was assigned to each of the three students daily to ensure the contract was being followed. The students were also asked to apologize to the victim's parents. The parents of the two girls granted permission to engage in a conversation with the parents of the student being bullied.

Instructional: The two students who were engaged in the bullying behavior were assigned Upstander Academy provided by the school counselor. Upstander Academy was a series of sessions designed to help the students learn to identify why they are engaging in these behaviors and what social and emotional skills they can utilize in lieu of engaging in bullying behaviors to hurt others they are upset at.

Reflective: The two female students had to conduct interviews with students and adults who had been bullied in the past and share their reflections with the administrative team.

Restorative: Based on their input from the student alternative discipline form, the students were assigned restitution in the form of providing three parent academy sessions in partnership with a teacher on the impact of bullying on teens, how students can get bullied online for parents, and what parents can do to help. After their sessions, they had to gather responses from parents.

Reflective: A circle was conducted at the end of the alternative discipline with the stakeholders involved to reflect on the process and ensure coexisting agreements would be followed.

 ## ALTERNATIVE DISCIPLINE CASE STUDY 5: INAPPROPRIATE LANGUAGE

A seventh-grade male student was asked several times by his English teacher to take out his journal and begin the writing prompt written on the board. Unbeknown to the teacher, this student was having a difficult time in all periods prior to her class period. After the majority of the class began their writing prompt, she gave one more directive to the student to take out his work and begin writing, or else he would be receiving a zero on the assignment. She unintentionally did so in a manner where other students sitting around the student were able to hear her comment to him. The student pushed his desk, almost knocking it over, and said "F@#K" this stupid assignment and "F@#K YOU" and stormed out of the classroom. This was not the first time this student got upset and mumbled underneath his breath to the teacher, but this was the first time it escalated to the words he used and his departure from the classroom. The teacher called to report the incident to the administrative team so they were aware a student was escalated and wandering around the school.

Knowing that suspending from school and specifically that class period for multiple days was not going to improve the situation between the teacher and student, the administrator wanted to try something different than the typical exclusionary response. The administrator knew the traditional response would feed into the repeated problem between the student and the teacher and not improve the behavior for the long term. After ensuring the student was given a safe space to de-escalate, the initial interview began. It was revealed through the initial interview the student had a horrible few days leading to this moment. His parents had announced they had to move again at the end of the school year and his girlfriend had broken up with him. He was also struggling to concentrate and was feeling extra triggered when asked to physically write out long paragraphs as an assignment in class. The administrator also checked in with the teacher and asked when the teacher would be willing to sit down and meet with the student—the three of them together. The teacher was also very offended and frustrated by how she was spoken to and wanted to ensure consequences would be put in place. The administrator assured her consequences would be put into place, but he wanted to ensure the consequences were meaningful and would help prevent the behavior from occurring again. The administrator also explained privileges would be earned back by the student as he demonstrated progress and completion of the alternative discipline contract.

Alternative Discipline

Reflective: An interview was conducted with the student using the student interview protocol.

Restorative: The administrator facilitated a restorative contract process with the student and teacher, allowing both sides an opportunity to have a voice and agree to a resolution.

Instructional: The student had to review the classroom agreement and complete a "write my new narrative" classroom contract in alignment with the classroom agreement. A weekly check-in section was part of the write your new narrative contract. As part of this contract, it was agreed upon by the student and teacher there would be a structured break process in place if he found himself feeling that frustrated again. In addition, the student had to develop a goal for his behavior that would be monitored by the student and teacher at least weekly.

Instructional: The student received four sessions from the school counselor on how to calm down when he perceives a situation to be unfair and how to ask for help when he needs it.

Instructional: The student had to research what would happen in the workplace if he spoke to the supervisor using that language and report back to the administrator.

Restorative: A classroom restitution agreement was established where the student "paid back" instructional time lost from the teacher due to this incident. The teacher and student agreed to three 30-minute time slots where the student would assist the teacher in the classroom during a time that worked for the teacher. In this case, the student and teacher agreed to three before-school time slots where the student helped the teacher organize the classroom, ensure tablets were charged, and so on.

Reflective: The student conducted an empathy interview with two students in the classroom about the incident to learn how his behavior also impacted the feeling of safety and security for others. This was conducted with adult supervision and with permission from the other students to participate.

AUTHORS' NOTE

Consistency and follow-through are critical when assigning alternatives. If any of the above alternatives highlighted through these case studies had an administrator tell a student they had to complete an assigned consequence but did not hold the student accountable to completing it, the results are as bad as doing nothing at all. The student will now not fear repeating their behavior because they know their administrator will not back up words with action. This is actually more counterproductive than suspension because now the student does not view the administrator as credible or consistent and all talk with no action. The administrator will also lose the credibility of the staff who were told the alternatives assigned but see that only parts of it were followed.

PART III

Alternative Discipline Menu by Common Behavior Incidents

6

Alternative Discipline Menu Introduction

This chapter will provide examples of alternative discipline from common discipline incidents in all school settings. It is designed to help you generate ideas for alternative discipline that will work at your school site. **Is the student returning to your school?** We understand some serious behavior incidents will result in a student's removal from a campus. The examples in this chapter are common suspendable incidents in which a student returns to school after serving a suspension. If the student is being placed in an alternative setting (i.e., Community Day School, Continuation School, Alternative Education, or Opportunity Program), the student should still receive the alternative discipline in their new setting as part of their transition, if possible.

This chapter is designed to bridge the gap between a traditional administrator to an innovative administrator when it comes to discipline. Student behavior will change when using these strategies as opposed to simply relying on suspension. When you see student behavior change, your beliefs around discipline will change along with it; then, you will begin thinking of your own alternative methods that will transform the culture of your school.

Alternative discipline resources will be provided after each behavior incident menu of suggestions. Resources used as examples in one menu aren't the only places they can be used and can be cross-referenced across other menu examples when appropriate or adjusted to meet appropriate grade-level needs. For example, the apology template is found in the Alternative Discipline Menu for Bullying; however, it can be applied as a restorative consequence in any number of behavior incidents. As you use this chapter to frame alternative discipline for incidents at your school, remember to include at least one restorative, one reflective, and one instructional example. Accountability for implementation of the assigned alternatives is key to its success. **Discipline assignments and supports need to be consistently in place and monitored to completion to get the positive outcomes you wish to see.** A lack of follow-through from the administrator assigning discipline will diminish student, staff, and stakeholder buy-in and create unintended negative outcomes. Our research has shown that a lack of administrator beliefs and inconsistency of implementation will lead to ineffective results. Administrators in such environments will say, "We tried using alternatives and they don't work." Consistent implementation from effective administrators has been proven to show tremendous success in changing student behavior. It's not that the alternatives don't work; it's that ineffective implementation, weak systems, or beliefs aren't in place to support them.

It is also important to archive what you have attempted to change in a student's behavior. It will also be helpful in demonstrating that the school has exhausted its resources to support a student behaviorally. If it comes to a Student Success Team or Individualized Education Plan meeting to problem solve next steps with the student, this will be important data to support decisions to move a student from perhaps a tier two to tier three behavior intervention. Documentation is also important to give a student continued support from grade to grade or school to school. As a student matriculates from an elementary setting to middle school to high school, it is critical for each new setting to have access to what the student has or has not responded to.

Create an alternative behavior toolkit (either a binder or electronic format) to reference for alternative discipline assignments. This will help you expand on the resources used in this book. As you transition to an innovative discipline administrator, you will learn what we refer to as the art of discipline, which will result in thinking differently when approaching behavior incidents at your school. Rather than being on discipline autopilot and assigning suspensions, you will think of alternative scenarios for incidents, create opportunities for students to learn from their behaviors, and connect the discipline to real-life consequences that change behaviors for the long term. Collaborate with your school psychologist, school counselor, behavior intervention specialist, district office behavior experts, general education and special education teachers, community resources, and any other school or district employees who have expertise in behavior to assist in establishing an effective behavior toolkit. In the next chapter, you will find the alternative discipline menu for the 13 most common suspendable behavior incidents in schools. **This second edition includes an additional section in Chapter 7 titled Universal Alternative Discipline Forms & Menu, which can be utilized for an array of behavior incidents.**

7A

Alternative Discipline Menu

Behavior Incident

BULLYING

Suggestions for Alternatives

Restorative: Student will complete a restorative contract with the other student, getting to the root of the problem and monitored by administration with six to eight weekly check-in points to determine if the contract agreed upon is being followed.

Restorative: Student will be assigned 10 days of restitution for the student who they were bullying (restitution to be completed during social time, before school, breaks, lunch, or after school). An adult "boss" or supervisor will be assigned to help supervise the restitution and assignment(s).

Instructional: Student will research bullying and tolerance and create a slide presentation (e.g., PowerPoint, Prezi, Google Slides) to teach other peers about bullying prevention (e.g., lessons on relationships, how behaviors impact others, what behaviors will help them with making friends, learning empathy).

Restorative: Apology letters will be written to all stakeholders impacted—other student, administration, and parent(s) of the other student.

Reflective: Student found bullying will be actively supervised to ensure they are following the contract (earning full school privileges back only after all consequences and assignments are completed).

Instructional: Student will be assigned six sessions of bullying prevention lessons, scenarios, and application opportunities.

Reflective: Student will complete a behavior exam to demonstrate understanding and application of learned skills.

Restorative: Students will revisit the restorative contract at least once a week for four weeks with an administrator or designee supervision.

Instructional: Communication and monitoring with parents of the students to work together to ensure the bullying is no longer taking place (providing parents with strategies to monitor and help at home).

Reflective: After 10 good days following the contract and schedule, the student bullying will get a few privileges back; in 10 more days, the student will receive complete privileges back but be required to check in on a biweekly basis with administration to ensure the bullying has stopped.

Restorative: Students will be assigned a joint project (e.g., creating an antibullying video for the school) with the supervision of the administrator or designee.

For the student being bullied (additional suggestions to consider):

- Establish a safe zone on campus for them to go to
- Check in with student throughout the day
- Supervision of the contract and expectations
- Possible counseling (e.g., strategies for them to cope)
- Possibly working with the student who bullied them on a common project (you would have to monitor and give them a safe zone to work together)

Apology Letter Template

Write an apology letter that includes the following components:

☐ Address the stakeholder(s) you have impacted due to your behavior

☐ Identify and own the behavior that put you in this position

☐ Acknowledge the hurt you may have caused due to your behavior

☐ Identify the function of your behavior

☐ Express your apology to those your behavior has impacted

☐ Provide three examples of what you have learned from this experience

☐ Provide three examples demonstrating what will prevent you from engaging in this type of behavior again

☐ Assure the stakeholder(s) this will never happen again

☐ Sign the letter as a contract to your apology

☐ Write five things you like and respect about the person you bullied; provide evidence to support each of the five

Project Assignment Template

Problem Behavior: Bullying

Possible Function of Behavior: Jealousy, lack of social skills

Date to Complete By: _____

Project Assignment

1. Research two local or national newspaper articles that highlight bullying and respond to the following writing prompts: What were commonalities between the articles? What are some ways to prevent bullying? What have you learned from this assignment?

   _____

   _____

   _____

2. Research laws on bullying. List three laws created to prevent bullying. Provide examples of how to follow the laws.

   _____

   _____

   _____

3. Develop a project to create bullying prevention awareness. Project needs to include the definition of bullying, ways to prevent bullying, and lessons learned.

   _____

   _____

   _____

Administrator Signature: _____

Stakeholder Signature(s): _____

Student(s) Signature: _____

Restorative Contract Monitoring Form (elementary grades)

Date of Check-In	How are we doing? ☺ ☹	Students' Signatures	Administrator or Designee Signatures
	Circle one: ☺ ☹		
	Circle one: ☺ ☹		
	Circle one: ☺ ☹		
	Circle one: ☺ ☹		
	Circle one: ☺ ☹		
	Circle one: ☺ ☹		
	Circle one: ☺ ☹		

Incentive when goal is met: If we can complete six to eight weeks of positive check-in ratings, we will get to have a special lunch with the administrator and each student can invite a friend.

Behavior Incident

 ## CYBERBULLYING

Suggestions for Alternatives

Instructional: Student will research federal laws related to cyberbullying, provide a summary of at least three identified laws, and present findings to the administrator.

Reflective: Student will write an article to submit to the school news or local news on how to help students stop cyberbullying.

Instructional: Student will complete six sessions with a designated employee to learn social skills to express feelings without using cyberbullying, which will include role-play practice opportunities.

Restorative: Student will complete a restorative contract between the students and daily check-ins with the administrator for six weeks.

Reflective: Student will create a pamphlet to help create awareness of cyberbullying based on research from cyberbullying case studies.

Restorative: Student will write apology letters to all stakeholders.

Reflective: The student will facilitate a student social media contract with the class or other students.

Instructional: Student will research the impacts of cyberbullying on students and their families and write a two-page paper explaining what was found and how to prevent this from happening.

Restorative: The student will assist the librarian, teacher, or computer technology assistant with keeping the school computers clean from any inappropriate content (10 days).

Instructional: The student will complete a book study/report on cyberbullying.

Social Media Exercise and Pledge

What is the purpose of social media (Facebook, Twitter, Instagram, etc.)?

_____

_____

What is cyberbullying?

_____

_____

Is bullying on social media against the law?

_____

_____

Do your messages or pictures disappear when you delete them?

_____

_____

What are five things you are committing to that will make sure cyberbullying does not happen?

1. _____

2. _____

3. _____

4. _____

5. _____

I pledge to do my part to stop cyberbullying. I pledge to always think before I post a message or picture that can hurt myself or others. I also pledge to help a friend by notifying an adult or the school if someone is being cyberbullied.

Rewrite the pledge:

_____

_____

_____

Signature: _____ Date: _____

Cyberbullying Practice Scenarios

Scenario 1: You are at a party where other students are pressuring you to post a picture on social media that would embarrass another student. You feel pressured to fit in with the students.

What would you do if you were in this situation to prevent cyberbullying?

_____

_____

_____

_____

Scenario 2: Students at school are creating fake online accounts so they can post mean comments on other student online accounts without anyone knowing it is them. They ask you to participate in this with them.

What would you do if you were in this situation to prevent cyberbullying?

_____

_____

_____

_____

Scenario 3: A student is dating someone you like. You feel angry at this person and want to make up a rumor and share it through as many online outlets as possible. Your friends are encouraging you to do so.

What would you do if you were in this situation to prevent cyberbullying?

_____

_____

_____

_____

Book Study/Report Template

Steps

1. Research books written about this topic
2. Check out a book
3. Read the book
4. Complete the following, aligned with the book you read:

   ❐ Summary of the book

   ❐ Lessons learned from the book

   ❐ Identify ways this book can help other students in similar situations

   ❐ Suggestions for preventing this type of problem behavior in the future based on examples from the book

   ❐ Commitment from the student to never engage in this type of behavior again

   ❐ Create a flyer identifying the value of this book

Behavior Incident

 # DRUG/ALCOHOL OFFENSE

Suggestions for Alternatives

Reflective: Meet with a school or community police officer and gather information on the consequences of engaging in this type of behavior in the community. Write a two-page paper sharing what you learned from the police officer.

Instructional: Student will help plan and organize with the designated administrator or school staff on a drug-free campaign for the student body.

Restorative: Write apology letters to all stakeholders.

Reflective: Interview the school nurse about the effects of drugs/alcohol on a child and write a one-page paper on what you learned from the interview.

Instructional: Research the dangers of underage drinking and the damage to the development of a child. Student will create a slide presentation and present it to the administrator and/or assigned classrooms/students.

Reflective: Student presents the research to a class (after proofed, as appropriate, by an administrator) with the student's parents present.

Instructional: Six to eight sessions of behavior lessons practicing how to stand up to peer pressure and how to make the right decisions. Students will practice through scenarios where they are expected to apply the law to demonstrate what they've learned.

Restorative: Student assigned 20 hours of community service. Loss of privileges until the completion of all community service hours.

Restorative: Develop a student contract.

Instructional: Research a drug and alcohol policy in a selected workplace environment. Summarize the policy in a one-page paper and be prepared to present key findings.

Alcohol Assignment

Assignment: Research the answers to the questions provided.

1. What are the effects of alcohol on teenagers and adults?

   _____

   _____

   _____

2. What can happen if you mix alcohol with other drugs?

   _____

   _____

   _____

3. What are some of the short-term and long-term effects of alcohol?

   _____

   _____

   _____

4. What are ways alcohol can keep you from reaching your goals?

   _____

   _____

   _____

5. What is the impact of alcohol abuse on family and friends?

   _____

   _____

   _____

6. What are the laws connected to alcohol?

   _____

   _____

   _____

7. What are some ways teachers and administrators can help prevent students from making poor decisions with alcohol?

   _____

   _____

   _____

8. What have you learned from this experience?

   _____

   _____

   _____

Law and Case Study Practice Worksheet

Assignment: Research three laws related to alcohol and drug offenses and summarize the laws.

Law:

_____

_____

Summary:

_____

_____

Law:

_____

_____

Summary:

_____

_____

Law:

_____

_____

Summary:

_____

_____

Read the case study and answer the questions.

Case Study: Jim and Joe have been best friends since the first grade. They strive for popularity at school and often test the boundaries of school rules. Jim called Joe on Sunday night to let him know he snuck some alcohol from a party his parents had the night before. The boys decide Jim is going to bring the beer he stole from the party to school the next day so they both can try it. At school, Jim brags that he brought alcohol and was showing it to other students. They went out at break to drink the beer, but before they took one sip, an adult on supervision heard about what they were doing and notified the administrator.

Case Study Questions

1. Have any laws been broken?

_____

_____

2. Why do you think the students behaved in the way that they did?

_____

_____

3. How do you think law enforcement would respond to this type of behavior?

_____

_____

4. Will the parents of these students be involved?

_____

_____

5. What do you think the students could have done instead?

_____

_____

6. What do you think is an appropriate consequence for these students?

_____

_____

7. What would help teach these students a lesson?

_____

_____

Drug and Alcohol Policy Assignment

Identify a workplace/employee to be researched (e.g., Target employee, engineer, doctor, teacher):

_____

Research a drug and alcohol policy in your selected workplace environment. Summarize the policy and answer the questions.

Summary of the policy:

_____

_____

_____

_____

_____

_____

_____

1. What would happen if alcohol or drug abuse is observed during work hours on company premises?

   _____

   _____

2. What are some apparent physical states of impairment in employees using drugs or alcohol during work hours?

   _____

   _____

3. What do you think is the mental state of a person using drugs or alcohol at work?

   _____

   _____

4. What are some changes in personal behavior that would otherwise be unexplainable?

_____

_____

5. Do you think the use of drugs and alcohol can deteriorate a person's work performance?

_____

_____

6. What kind of accidents can occur in a workplace due to the use of drugs and alcohol?

_____

_____

7. What is a consequence for an employee who tests positive for drugs or alcohol in the workplace?

_____

_____

Behavior Incident

 FIGHT

Suggestions for Alternatives

Restorative: The administrator will conduct a conflict resolution using a restorative approach to get to the root cause of the fight. This conflict resolution will be ongoing and occur three or four times to ensure the conflict is resolved over the next few weeks.

Restorative: The students will create and monitor a contract together under the supervision of an administrator for at least six weeks.

Instructional: Students will go through at least six sessions of hands-off academy behavior teaching lessons where they will learn and practice strategies before applying them to scenarios demonstrating mastery of learning.

Reflective: Students will be required to take an exit behavior exam demonstrating what they have learned from this experience prior to resuming full privileges on campus.

Instructional: Students will prepare a lesson and teach it to younger students or peers about the importance of solving problems appropriately.

Restorative: Students will have to write an apology letter to any stakeholders affected as a result of this behavior incident.

Reflective: Students will stay on a structured schedule until the completion of all requirements.

Restorative Contract

Date of Meeting: _____

Disputants

_____   _____   _____

_____   _____   _____

Referral Source

Administrator   Teacher   Student   Self   Other: _____

Conflict Information

What is the conflict about? _____

_____

_____

_____

_____

1. Did we recognize an injustice/violation?   Yes   No   Other: _____

2. Did we restore equity?   Yes   No

   Apology for injustices/violations: Yes   No

   Nothing beyond this meeting is necessary: Yes   No   Other: _____

3. Future Intentions (Agreement/Contract)

   We agree to prevent this problem from happening again by: _____

_____

_____

_____

_____

_____

_____

Student Signatures: _____   _____   _____

(Continued)

(Continued)

4. Follow-Up Meeting

We agree to meet again for a follow-up meeting.

Follow-Up Meeting Date: _____

Follow-Up Results: _____

_____

_____

_____

_____

_____

Student Signatures: _____ _____ _____

Behavior Exam

1. What happened that put you in this position?

   _____

   _____

   _____

   _____

2. What would you have done differently if you could go back and change what happened?

   _____

   _____

   _____

   _____

3. What did you learn from this experience? Provide three examples.

   _____

   _____

   _____

   _____

4. How can you assure the administration that you will not be a part of an incident such as this ever again? Provide three reasons.

   _____

   _____

   _____

   _____

5. How will you ensure that the student who was the victim of your behavior will not have to worry about you bothering them anymore? Provide three examples.

   _____

   _____

   _____

   _____

Hands-Off Academy: Weekly Self-Monitoring Form

Student Name: _____

Behaviors: How Well Did I . . .	Previous Week	
Show respect to adults and students	Circle one:	Good Fair Poor
Keep my hands to myself	Circle one:	Good Fair Poor

What worked for you? _____

_____

What didn't work for you? _____

_____

Contract for This Week

I, _____, will work on _____ this week in order to meet my behavior goal.

Administrator Signature: _____

Student Signature: _____

Behavior Incident

FIRE RELATED

Suggestions for Alternatives

Instructional: Student will contact the local fire department to research fire safety courses available to students. If available, have the student participate in the course and present what he learned to classmates or younger students.

Restorative: Student will write apology letters to all stakeholders.

Instructional: Student will interview and shadow the custodian for a week and will write a two-page paper describing the role of the custodian and how this type of behavior impacts the custodian's work.

Restorative: Student will complete restitution with the custodian decided by the administrator.

Reflective: Student will prepare and present a fire safety slide presentation.

Reflective: Student will interview a local family or someone they know who has lost their belongings or been impacted as the result of a fire and write a two-page reflection on what this experience has taught them.

Reflective: Student will research and write an essay on the consequences associated with fire-connected acts within the community.

Restorative: Student will research volunteer opportunities to help families who have lost valuables and so on in fire-related incidents.

Shadow Log

Assignment: Student will shadow a designated adult for one week. The student will log what they learned from the experience and will write a two-page reflection paper summarizing what they learned.

Date	Who Did You Shadow?	What Did You Learn?	Designated Adult Signature

Custodian Interview Questions

Assignment: Interview a custodian and summarize responses in a two-page reflection sheet.

1. What does your job entail on campus?

_____

_____

_____

_____

2. What are your experiences with fire-related incidents on campus?

_____

_____

_____

_____

3. How does a student engaging in a fire-related incident affect your work day?

_____

_____

_____

_____

4. What is in place to keep the school safe from fire-related incidents?

_____

_____

_____

_____

5. What do you think students can do to help prevent these types of incidents at school?

_____

_____

_____

_____

Fire-Related Slide Presentation Assignment Template

Date: _____

Student to complete and present a slide presentation that includes the following components:

- ☐ Topic: Fire-related incidents
- ☐ Overall question(s) to answer through research or educational course related to fire safety:

  What did you learn about fire safety that would be helpful to others?

  What are some tips to prevent fire-related incidents at school?

  What are some awareness activities that can help schools prevent fire-related incidents?

- ☐ Cite five research resources:

  _____

  _____

  _____

  _____

  _____

  _____

  _____

  _____

  _____

  _____

- ☐ Negative outcomes of engaging in this behavior
- ☐ Positive outcomes of not engaging in this behavior
- ☐ Methods to prevent this behavior in the future
- ☐ Final answer to the original overall question

Administrator Signature: _____

Student Signature: _____

Behavior Incident

INAPPROPRIATE LANGUAGE

Suggestions for Alternatives

Instructional: Student will be provided practice opportunities on how to rephrase inappropriate language to appropriate language.

Instructional: Student will teach younger grades appropriate language rules in school.

Reflective: Student will interview others around campus on how inappropriate language makes them feel.

Reflective: Student will complete an essay on how inappropriate language can affect their future in a workplace or within the community.

Reflective: Student will identify 10 positive appropriate words for each negative/inappropriate word used.

Instructional: Student will research the meaning of the language used (when appropriate) and create a presentation sharing the history of the words.

Instructional: Student will complete six sessions of behavior lessons on self-control.

Restorative: Student will write apology letters to students and others offended by the language.

Restorative: Student will be placed on a language contract.

Reflective: Student will complete a respect reflection sheet.

Respect Reflection Sheet

Name: _____

Write a plan on how you can be more respectful:

_____

_____

_____

_____

_____

_____

What happens when you are not respectful?

_____

_____

_____

_____

_____

_____

What makes you a respectful person?

_____

_____

_____

_____

_____

_____

Write three school rules that help everyone to be respectful:

_____

_____

_____

_____

_____

_____

_____

_____

What consequences should be in place for students who are not respectful?

_____

_____

_____

_____

_____

_____

_____

_____

Give me some examples of things that *are* and *are not* respectful:

_____   _____

_____   _____

_____   _____

_____   _____

_____   _____

On another page, make a poster about being respectful.

Inappropriate Language Worksheet

Write down the inappropriate language used:

_____

_____

_____

Write three other ways you can communicate what you meant appropriately:

1. _____

2. _____

3. _____

Write why these words are inappropriate:

_____

_____

_____

Write five positive words in place of the word(s) used toward the other student:

1. _____

2. _____

3. _____

4. _____

5. _____

Behavior Incident

PROPERTY DAMAGE

Suggestions for Alternatives

Reflective: Interview the student to figure out the reason that student caused the damage.

Restorative: Student will apologize to the custodian and other stakeholders in person or through an apology letter.

Restorative: Student will be assigned restitution for 15 days or administrator-decided length of time based on the damage. The custodian or another stakeholder will supervise the student and sign off on restitution work and attitude of the student during restitution. The student will write a thank-you letter after the completion of restitution to show their appreciation and understanding of this life lesson.

Instructional: Student will research the cost of damage and work with stakeholders to develop a workplan for correcting the damage. The action plan will be presented to the administrator and stakeholders.

Instructional: Student will complete six to eight sessions of behavior academy or teaching opportunity, providing student scenarios to help the student see the effects of their behavior on others and to learn self-control skills.

Instructional: Administrator will print examples of local stores that have been vandalized for the student to research and learn the impact vandalism has on others. Student will write an essay demonstrating empathy with evidence from the local examples.

Instructional: Student will research adult consequences for property damage and write a one-page reflection on how this type of behavior can impact a person's life in a negative way.

Restorative: Develop a contract with monitoring by the administration for at least six to eight weeks.

Property Damage Audit

Assignment: Research the cost of damage and work with assigned stakeholder to develop an action plan for improvement. Write a two-page paper describing your experience with this damage audit and the completion of the damage cleanup.

Property Damage Cleanup Action Plan

Action Type			
Finding			
Root Cause			
Proposed Action			
Due Date		Task Assigned To	
Completion Date		Task Approved By	
Final Action			
Action Effectiveness			
Evaluation Date		Task Approved By	

Property Damage Practice Scenarios

Scenario 1: Your friends are bored over the weekend. One friend suggests going to vandalize your school. All of your friends seem to be on board with this plan.

What would you do if you were in this situation to prevent property damage?

_____

_____

_____

_____

Scenario 2: You know that no one is monitoring the bathrooms after lunch. You are mad at a student and want to write degrading messages about them in the bathroom.

What would you do if you were in this situation to prevent property damage?

_____

_____

_____

_____

Scenario 3: The teacher you do not like leaves the classroom unsupervised. You know you have access to do as you wish to her classroom items. Your friends are pressuring you to do so.

What would you do if you were in this situation to prevent property damage?

_____

_____

_____

_____

Restitution Monitoring Sheet

Amount of restitution assigned: _____

Restitution description: _____

What was the behavior that resulted in restitution? _____

Supervisor name: _____

Date/Restitution Amount Served	Did I Complete My Assigned Restitution With Quality Effort? (Yes or No) Supervisor Signature	Did I Complete My Assigned Restitution With a Good Attitude? (Yes or No) Supervisor Signature

After the completion of your restitution, write a one-page reflection to your restitution supervisor thanking them for the opportunity and sharing with them what you have learned from this experience.

Behavior Incident

REPEATED CLASSROOM DISRUPTIONS

Suggestions for Alternatives

Restorative: Student will be placed on a classroom contract developed with the teacher and monitored on a daily basis.

Restorative: Student will be placed on a restorative agreement with the teacher and coordinated with the support of an administrator to ensure the relationship is restored.

Restorative: Student will write an apology letter to the teacher.

Reflective: Student will be placed on check-in/check-out targeted intervention designed for additional structure and increased positive adult interaction for six to eight weeks (Todd et al., 2008).

Instructional: Student will receive six to eight sessions of behavior academy lessons to teach the student how to follow classroom rules and contract.

Restorative: Student will complete restitution in the classroom or around school (based on teacher and administration).

Reflective: Student will complete a behavior exam for the student to apply learned skills.

Reflective: Student will have an Alternative Zone to complete work and practice replacement behaviors learned in behavior academies.

Reflective: Student will complete a "Write 'Your New Story' Prompt" form and present what they wrote with the teacher and administrator.

Check-In/Check-Out Monitoring Form

Date: _____	Be Respectful	Be Safe	Work Peacefully	Strive for Excellence	Follow Directions	Teacher Initials
8:45 – A.M. Break	0　1　2	0　1　2	0　1　2	0　1　2	0　1　2	
A.M. Break – 12:00	0　1　2	0　1　2	0　1　2	0　1　2	0　1　2	
12:00 – Lunch	0　1　2	0　1　2	0　1　2	0　1　2	0　1　2	
Lunch – End of Day	0　1　2	0　1　2	0　1　2	0　1　2	0　1　2	

Total Points: _____ Possible Points: 40   Today: ____%   **Goal: 70% or 28/40 points**

Date: _____	Be Respectful	Be Safe	Work Peacefully	Strive for Excellence	Follow Directions	Teacher Initials
8:45 – A.M. Break	0　1　2	0　1　2	0　1　2	0　1　2	0　1　2	
A.M. Break – 12:00	0　1　2	0　1　2	0　1　2	0　1　2	0　1　2	
12:00 – Lunch	0　1　2	0　1　2	0　1　2	0　1　2	0　1　2	
Lunch – End of Day	0　1　2	0　1　2	0　1　2	0　1　2	0　1　2	

Total Points: _____ Possible Points: 40   Today: ____%   **Goal: 70% or 28/40 points**

Date: _____	Be Respectful	Be Safe	Work Peacefully	Strive for Excellence	Follow Directions	Teacher Initials
8:45 – A.M. Break	0　1　2	0　1　2	0　1　2	0　1　2	0　1　2	
A.M. Break – 12:00	0　1　2	0　1　2	0　1　2	0　1　2	0　1　2	
12:00 – End of Day	0　1　2	0　1　2	0　1　2	0　1　2	0　1　2	

Total Points: _____ Possible Points: 30   Today: ____%   **Goal: 70% or 21/30 points**

Date: _____	Be Respectful	Be Safe	Work Peacefully	Strive for Excellence	Follow Directions	Teacher Initials
8:45 – A.M. Break	0　1　2	0　1　2	0　1　2	0　1　2	0　1　2	
A.M. Break – 12:00	0　1　2	0　1　2	0　1　2	0　1　2	0　1　2	
12:00 – Lunch	0　1　2	0　1　2	0　1　2	0　1　2	0　1　2	
Lunch – End of Day	0　1　2	0　1　2	0　1　2	0　1　2	0　1　2	

Total Points: _____ Possible Points: 40   Today: ____%   **Goal: 70% or 28/40 points**

Date: _____	Be Respectful	Be Safe	Work Peacefully	Strive for Excellence	Follow Directions	Teacher Initials
8:45 – A.M. Break	0　1　2	0　1　2	0　1　2	0　1　2	0　1　2	
A.M. Break – 12:00	0　1　2	0　1　2	0　1　2	0　1　2	0　1　2	
12:00 – Lunch	0　1　2	0　1　2	0　1　2	0　1　2	0　1　2	
Lunch – End of Day	0　1　2	0　1　2	0　1　2	0　1　2	0　1　2	

Total Points: _____ Possible Points: 40   Today: ____%   **Goal: 70% or 28/40 points**

0 = Poor   1 = Fair   2 = Great Job!

Write "Your New Story" Prompt

Name:_____ Date:_____

Who am I . . .

_____

_____

_____

_____

_____

_____

_____

What are some poor choices I have made in the past at school (*my old story*)?

_____

_____

_____

_____

_____

_____

_____

What do I want to see for myself (*my new story*) when it comes to behavior and academics in school?

_____

_____

_____

_____

_____

_____

_____

(Continued)

(Continued)

How do I plan on making this *new story* come true?

_____

_____

_____

_____

_____

_____

_____

What help do I need to make this *new story* come true?

_____

_____

_____

_____

_____

_____

_____

Student signature of commitment to *My New Story:*_____

Alternative Zone

Beginning Date: _____   Ending Date: _____

This Alternative Zone is designed to give the student an opportunity to practice their learned replacement behaviors from behavior academy and to provide an Alternative Zone that can be utilized through teacher and/or student request to go to a safe space to complete organized assignments with adult supervision instead of disruptive behavior escalating in class. The goal is for the student to decrease the number of times they go into this Alternative Zone location.

> **Important note to consider throughout the day: Alternative Zone (designated location with structured assignments and designated adult support)**
>
> If the student is disrupting teaching or about to engage in attention-seeking behavior with the teacher (power struggle), the teacher will send the student with a red folder to the designated location. The teacher is to make a phone call to the office with a selected code for someone to come help with the situation if the teacher perceives this will trigger the student's behavior.
>
> If the student is at a point where they need to be removed, the following are examples of structured assignments to be completed: Read Accelerated Reader book (take notes, pass a quiz), online math intervention (40 minutes), online reading intervention (40 minutes), math facts practice, essay on appropriate behavior, or any incomplete work the teacher wants completed.

Progress Monitoring

(Administrator to fill out and track the number of times in each day the student went to the Alternative Zone)

Dates	How many times did student go to the Alternative Zone?	Was the plan followed with fidelity today?			
Week:		Student	Teacher	Parent	Admin
Monday					
Tuesday					
Wednesday					
Thursday					
Friday					

Behavior Incident

 ## SEXUAL HARASSMENT

Suggestions for Alternatives

Restorative: A restorative agreement will be completed between the students.

Restorative: Student will write apology letters to all stakeholders.

Reflective: Student will interview important women in their life and ask how they would feel if someone sexually harassed them. Student will present what they learned to the administrator.

Instructional: Student will research the district handbook description on sexual harassment and identify a sexual harassment policy in a work environment. Student will write an essay describing what was learned and the consequences connected to engaging in these types of behaviors within the community.

Instructional: Student is assigned four sessions with a designated school employee to role-play appropriate ways of seeking peer attention from other students. In these sessions, student will be provided scenarios and taught strategies to handle them appropriately.

Restorative: Student will meet with the victim in a safe, supervised place with the administrator present to share what was learned from this experience and how it will not continue.

Reflective: Student will create an individual behavior contract identifying their commitment to changing their behavior.

Instructional: Student will visit the U.S. Department of Justice website to research prevention on violence against women and present findings and laws to the administrator.

Reflective: Student will be given a structured schedule with check-ins set up for six to eight weeks with the administrator.

Student Contract Template

Date of Contract: _____

Contract Monitoring Dates:

_____ _____ _____ _____ _____ _____

I, _____, am writing this contract to ensure that I will not engage in the behavior that resulted in hurting myself or others again. The behavior I was engaged in included _____, and I hurt _____ _____ by engaging in this behavior. I am going to take the following actions to ensure I will never engage in this behavior again:

Identified Actions

1. _____

2. _____

3. _____

4. _____

5. _____

I will ensure I am following my identified actions by:

_____

_____

I will monitor how I am doing with my contract by:

_____

_____

I will need help with the following to make sure I follow my identified actions:

_____

_____

I believe the following needs to take place if I do not follow my contract:

_____

_____

Student Signature: _____

Administrator Signature: _____

Project Assignment Template

Problem behavior (e.g., sexual harassment): _____ _____

Possible function of behavior (e.g., attention seeking, lack of social skills): _____

_____

Date to complete by: _____

Project Assignment

1. Research two sexual harassment descriptions or policies and respond to the following writing prompts: What were commonalities between the policies? What are some ways to prevent sexual harassment? What have you learned from this assignment?

_____

_____

_____

_____

2. Research sexual harassment laws. List three laws created to prevent sexual harassment in the workplace. Provide examples of how to follow the laws.

_____

_____

_____

_____

3. Develop a project to create sexual harassment prevention awareness. Project needs to include the following: definition of sexual harassment, ways to prevent sexual harassment, and lessons learned.

_____

_____

_____

_____

Administrator Signature: _____

Stakeholder Signature(s): _____

Student(s) Signature: _____

Sample Structured Schedule

Beginning Date: _____   Ending Date:_____

Where am I supposed to report and what am I doing during the following times of the school day.

Before-School Check-In: _____

Class: _____

Morning Recess: _____

Class: _____

Lunch and Lunch Recess: _____

After-School Check-Out: _____

Date	Did I check in this morning? (Yes or No) Administrator or Designee Signature	Did I follow my schedule today with no problems? (Yes or No) Administrator or Designee Signature
10 pass days earns privileges back to the student		

Behavior Incident

 # SUBSTITUTE TEACHER

Suggestions for Alternatives

Restorative: Student will write an apology letter to the substitute teacher.

Restorative: Student will complete classroom restitution with the administrator, teacher, and student.

Reflective: Student will write the rules and expectations of the class when a substitute is present.

Instructional: Student will create an assignment for their classmates to participate in. The assignment will be led by the student on the topic of appropriate ways to behave with a substitute teacher in class.

Instructional: Student will research substitute teacher job descriptions and present the requirements to the administrator.

Reflective: Student will interview a substitute teacher and write a one-page reflection of the challenges and opportunities that come with substitute teaching.

Reflective: Student will interview five students on appropriate ways to behave when a substitute teacher is in class and prepare a handout that highlights 10 ways to behave with a substitute teacher.

Restorative: The student will facilitate a classroom substitute teacher contract discussion that will be reviewed the morning any substitute teacher enters the classroom.

Restorative: Student will be assigned five mornings of welcoming a substitute teacher on campus (in any grade), where the student is required to share school behavior expectations and rules and walk them to their classroom after the check-in.

Classroom Substitute Teacher Contract

Assignment: The student is to guide classmates through the following questions, then develop a classroom contract with the collected information signed by all students and posted in the classroom. The student is to review the substitute teacher contract with their class prior to having a substitute teacher in class to reinforce the contract.

Facilitating Questions

- How should we behave when a substitute teacher is in our class?

- What are some behaviors that should not take place when we have a substitute teacher?

- What does it look like to show respect to the substitute teacher?

- What can we commit to doing when we have a substitute teacher?

- Why is it important to treat a substitute teacher in this way?

- How can we make sure we are respecting this contract?

Substitute Teacher Interview Questions

Assignment: Interview a substitute teacher and write a two-page reflection addressing the following questions using evidence from the interview. Provide a copy of the reflection to the teacher, interviewed substitute teacher, and administrator.

1. What are some challenges of being a substitute teacher?

2. What are some opportunities of being a substitute teacher?

3. How should students behave when they have a substitute teacher?

Substitute Teacher Interview Questions

• Why did you get into substitute teaching?

• How do you expect students to behave when you are substitute teaching?

• Have you experienced disrespectful students while you were substitute teaching?

• How do you feel when students are not following classroom rules when you are substitute teaching?

• Have you had positive experiences substitute teaching?

• What would be your ideal classroom to substitute for?

Develop three additional questions to ask the substitute teacher:

1. _____

2. _____

3. _____

Substitute Welcoming Monitoring Chart

Assignment: Five mornings of welcoming a substitute teacher on campus, where the student is required to share school behavior expectations and rules before walking them to their classroom after the check-in. Provide a one-page reflection of this experience to the administrator after all five days of substitute welcoming committee time is completed.

Student Name: _____

Date	Substitute teacher name and classroom subbing in	Substitute teacher signature after being provided with an overview of the behavior expectations and rules and walked to the classroom	Administrator or designee signature

Behavior Incident

 TECHNOLOGY OFFENSE

Suggestions for Alternatives

Reflective: Student will review the school handbook or provided technology rules/policies and write a one-page reflection on the appropriate ways to use technology.

Restorative: Student will be assigned to assist the site technician or designated teacher on campus with technology support for four weeks during recess/break/lunch. Student will have loss of privileges until restitution is completed.

Reflective: Student will write a two-page paper on how to use technology appropriately, specifically referencing incidents where students abused technology and the impact that abuse had on the school's ability to make technology accessible to all students.

Instructional: Student will develop a slide presentation to educate other students on the appropriate use of technology.

Restorative: Student will develop a technology contract that is monitored by the student and administration to ensure this will not happen again.

Reflective: Student will undergo a daily technology check-in and check-out for four to six weeks to ensure there has not been any inappropriate searches or use.

Instructional: Student will work with an administrator or assigned teacher on a technology lesson for teachers, helping them see ways students can abuse technology so they are prepared to be proactive. Student will present at a staff meeting or other approved time for teacher professional development. This presentation may also be created in a webinar or video format.

Slide Presentation Assignment Template

Date: _____

Student to complete and present a slide presentation that includes the following components:

❑ Topic (e.g., student aggression, cyberbullying, theft):

_____

❑ Overall question to answer through research (e.g., How do we prevent technology offenses in school? How can we help teachers and administrators become aware of technology offenses? How can we help teachers and administrators become preventive when using technology in their classrooms?)

❑ Six examples of the resources used to prepare this presentation, along with evidence:

_____

_____

_____

_____

_____

_____

❑ Negative outcomes of engaging in this behavior

❑ Positive outcomes of not engaging in this behavior

❑ Methods to prevent this behavior in the future

❑ Final answer to the overall question

Administrator Signature: _____

Student Signature: _____

Reflection Paper Template

Assignment: Review the school handbook or provided technology rules/policies and write a one-page reflection on how to use technology appropriately. The completed reflection will be approved by the administrator and must include the following components:

❑ Describe the behavior that resulted in the misuse of technology.

❑ Describe what you could have done instead to avoid being in this position.

❑ Summarize the information provided to you for review.

❑ Provide three example scenarios of inappropriate technology offenses in schools and provide an explanation of how to prevent these types of technology offenses from occurring.

❑ Provide suggestions and tips for teachers and administrators on how to prevent technology offenses in schools.

❑ Describe how you plan to avoid inappropriate uses of technology in the future.

❑ Describe what you learned from this experience.

Technology Contract Template

I, _____, was engaged in using technology inappropriately, which resulted in a consequence at school. I understand I made a poor decision by engaging in this behavior and, therefore, I commit to the following to ensure that I will never participate in this type of behavior again:

1. _____

2. _____

3. _____

4. _____

5. _____

I am committing to monitor my technology contract on a weekly basis with the designated school faculty member assigned to ensure my contract is being honored.

Week of . . .	Did I follow my contract? (Yes or No) School Designee Signature
Week 1	
Week 2	
Week 3	
Week 4	
Week 5	
Week 6	

Student Signature: _____

Administrator Signature: _____

School Designee Signature: _____

Behavior Incident

 # THEFT

Suggestions for Alternatives

Reflective: Interview the student to identify the root of why the student stole the item.

Restorative: Provide an opportunity for the student who stole to apologize to the person(s) they stole from.

Reflective: Student will undergo morning and after-school check-ins with administration to ensure there are no stolen items leaving the campus. Process is approved by parents/guardians to continue for six to eight weeks.

Instructional: Student will research the average amount of community service assigned to an adult who steals in the community. Student will write a one-page reflection on findings and a community service proposal to be followed during restitution on campus.

Restorative: Student will complete community service/restitution on campus. The time of service will be aligned to the cost of stolen item. Student will have loss of privileges until community service and assignments are completed.

Instructional: Student will complete six sessions of behavior academies or opportunities focused on appropriate ways to earn what they want in school, home, and community.

Reflective: A classroom behavior contract will be developed with the teacher. It will be monitored on a daily and weekly basis.

Reflective: Student will be assigned a mentor on campus to provide support for the student with weekly check-ins with the mentor to ensure student is on track. Student is encouraged to provide feedback to a mentor who they respect.

Reflective: School will work with parents to provide family support if this is a common behavior happening at school, home, and community. Student will be assigned 10 days of journal entries that will include parent/guardian input.

Instructional: The student will write an essay on the importance of trust, with evidence demonstrating learning from this experience. The assignment will be signed off by the teacher and administration.

Community Service Form

Student Name: _____ Grade: _____

Date Service Begins: _____

Hours or Days Assigned:

_____ Total hours of service assigned

_____ Total days of service assigned

Community Service Job Description:

_____

_____

Community Service Supervisor: _____

Date	Location of Service	Time or Days (e.g., 3 Hours or a Full Day)	Staff Initials	Additional Comments

At the completion of service, student will submit a reflection on what they learned from this experience, and an administrator, supervisor, parent, and student need to sign this document.

Administrator Signature: _____

Community Service Supervisor Signature: _____

Parent Signature: _____

Student Signature: _____

Check-In Monitoring Form

Date	Morning: Did I Have Anything in My Possession That Did Not Belong to Me? (Yes or No) Staff Initials	Afternoon: Did I Have Anything in My Possession That Did Not Belong to Me? (Yes or No) Staff Initials

Student Interview Questions: Theft

- Explain what took place from your side of the story.

- What made you take the item?

- Did you feel bad about taking the item?

- Did you ever consider returning the item?

- Do you think people have lost trust in you due to your behavior?

- What are you going to do to earn trust back?

- Has anyone stolen anything from you before? If yes, how did it make you feel?

- What do you think is an appropriate consequence for your behavior?

- Have you stolen items before?

- What type of help do you think you need to stop you from taking items from others?

- What do you think would happen if you got caught stealing something in the community?

- What are your plans to restore the relationship with the person(s) you stole from?

- Do you have any questions for me?

Behavior Incident

 # TRUANCY

Suggestions for Alternatives

Restorative: Student will be assigned a job at school with a designated supervisor for six weeks.

Restorative: Student will receive community service hours for the amount of school missed.

Instructional: Student will receive six to eight sessions of behavior lessons targeting organization, time management, and motivation.

Reflective: Student is required to have daily check-ins with designated school personnel.

Instructional: Student will research how truancy (absenteeism) can impact a career as an adult.

Instructional: Student will research and develop tips to prevent truancy that will be used as a guide for other students.

Reflective: A truancy contract will be developed with student input and monitored daily.

Truancy Progress Monitoring Sheet

Week of	Monday	Tuesday	Wednesday	Thursday	Friday	Point total	Did I meet my goal this week? (Yes or No)
Week 1	On time **Yes (1) or No (0)** Work completion progress **Yes (1) or No (0)**	On time **Yes (1) or No (0)** Work completion progress **Yes (1) or No (0)**	On time **Yes (1) or No (0)** Work completion progress **Yes (1) or No (0)**	On time **Yes (1) or No (0)** Work completion progress **Yes (1) or No (0)**	On time **Yes (1) or No (0)** Work completion progress **Yes (1) or No (0)**		
Week 2	On time **Yes (1) or No (0)** Work completion progress **Yes (1) or No (0)**	On time **Yes (1) or No (0)** Work completion progress **Yes (1) or No (0)**	On time **Yes (1) or No (0)** Work completion progress **Yes (1) or No (0)**	On time **Yes (1) or No (0)** Work completion progress **Yes (1) or No (0)**	On time **Yes (1) or No (0)** Work completion progress **Yes (1) or No (0)**		
Week 3	On time **Yes (1) or No (0)** Work completion progress **Yes (1) or No (0)**	On time **Yes (1) or No (0)** Work completion progress **Yes (1) or No (0)**	On time **Yes (1) or No (0)** Work completion progress **Yes (1) or No (0)**	On time **Yes (1) or No (0)** Work completion progress **Yes (1) or No (0)**	On time **Yes (1) or No (0)** Work completion progress **Yes (1) or No (0)**		
Week 4	On time **Yes (1) or No (0)** Work completion progress **Yes (1) or No (0)**	On time **Yes (1) or No (0)** Work completion progress **Yes (1) or No (0)**	On time **Yes (1) or No (0)** Work completion progress **Yes (1) or No (0)**	On time **Yes (1) or No (0)** Work completion progress **Yes (1) or No (0)**	On time **Yes (1) or No (0)** Work completion progress **Yes (1) or No (0)**		
Week 5	On time **Yes (1) or No (0)** Work completion progress **Yes (1) or No (0)**	On time **Yes (1) or No (0)** Work completion progress **Yes (1) or No (0)**	On time **Yes (1) or No (0)** Work completion progress **Yes (1) or No (0)**	On time **Yes (1) or No (0)** Work completion progress **Yes (1) or No (0)**	On time **Yes (1) or No (0)** Work completion progress **Yes (1) or No (0)**		
Week 6	On time **Yes (1) or No (0)** Work completion progress **Yes (1) or No (0)**	On time **Yes (1) or No (0)** Work completion progress **Yes (1) or No (0)**	On time **Yes (1) or No (0)** Work completion progress **Yes (1) or No (0)**	On time **Yes (1) or No (0)** Work completion progress **Yes (1) or No (0)**	On time **Yes (1) or No (0)** Work completion progress **Yes (1) or No (0)**		

Note: 8/10 points in a week = end of the day and end of the week small student-selected incentive from administrator

Behavior Worksheet: Time Management Skills

What is the definition of time management?

- How do you think time management is related to your truancy difficulties?

- What are factors preventing you from being on time and at school?

- What are factors contributing to you not getting to school on time?

- What are some ways to improve your attendance and tardiness?

- What can a school staff member help you with in order to improve your truancy?

Research the following and write a summary for each:

1. Research time management skills and write a summary of how you plan on implementing these learned skills.

2. Research what would happen to you if you were continuously late to your job in your future career, and write a summary about what you plan to do to prevent this from happening to you.

3. Research ways to keep up with your school workload, and write a summary of how you plan on utilizing school resources to catch up.

Student Contract Template

Truancy Contract Sample

Date of Contract: _____

Monitoring Dates: _____ _____ _____ _____ _____

I, _____, am writing this contract to ensure that I will improve my truancy. The truancy behavior I was engaged in that resulted in this contract includes _____. This behavior has hurt my educational progress by _____. I am going to take the following actions to ensure I will improve my truancy:

Identified Actions

1. _____

2. _____

3. _____

4. _____

5. _____

I will ensure I am following my identified actions by:

_____

_____

I will monitor how I am doing with my contract by:

_____

_____

I will need help with the following to make sure I adhere to my identified actions:

_____

_____

I believe the following needs to take place if I do not honor this contract:

_____

_____

Student Signature: _____

Administrator Signature: _____

7B

Universal Alternative Discipline Forms & Menu

In this section, we have added new universal alternative discipline forms and strategies that can be utilized for multiple types of behavior incidents.

Menu

Behavior Reflection/Solution Sheet

Complete the solution section for the prompt(s) you responded yes to.

Reflection Behavior		Solution (What is one thing I can do?)
Do I feel tired?	Yes/No	
Do I feel angry?	Yes/No	
Do I feel jealous?	Yes/No	
Do I feel mistreated?	Yes/No	
Do I want something I cannot have?	Yes/No	
Do I feel out of control?	Yes/No	
Do I feel unmotivated?	Yes/No	
Do I feel like no one cares?	Yes/No	
Do I feel frustrated?	Yes/No	
Do I feel overwhelmed?	Yes/No	
Do I feel alone?	Yes/No	
Do I feel like I am going to fail?	Yes/No	
Do I feel . . . Yes/No		
Do I feel . . . Yes/No		
Do I feel . . . Yes/No		
Do I feel . . . Yes/No		

Apology Letter to Self

Dear Self,

I am sorry for . . .

The behavior I engaged in was wrong because . . .

This behavior has impacted others because . . .

I accept full responsibility for my behaviors demonstrated by . . .

Moving forward, I will . . .

I am going to forgive myself by . . .

Sincerely,

Student-Developed Interview Questions Protocol

Who are you interviewing and why:

Develop at least five questions to ask your interviewee relevant to your behavior incident.

Interview Questions:	Response
1.	
2.	
3.	
4.	
5.	
Summarize key learnings from the interview:	
Interviewee signature:	Administrator signature:

Write a thank-you letter including:

Thanking the person for letting you interview them, summarize what you learned, and acknowledge what your commitment will be to move forward from this setback.

Class Pass Agreement Form

Class pass agreement allows a student to utilize a structured break system agreed upon with the adult(s). A designated signal or a physical class pass card may be utilized by the student to help them calmly remove themselves from a situation to have a safe, designated space to complete an assignment, task, or apply a regulation strategy.

Date and time class pass was utilized	Task/assignment/ regulation strategy	What location and designated staff provides support?	Task/assignment/ regulation strategy completed (Yes or No)	Utilized class pass appropriately (i.e., correct location, checked in with assigned adult, and worked on either task or assignment and/or practiced regulation strategy) (Yes or No) Designated class pass adult designee initials required

(Continued)

Student Class Pass Agreement Self-Monitoring Sheet

Weekly appropriate class pass usage goal:

How many times did I use the class pass each day? Use a tally to show how many times class pass was utilized.

Monday	Tuesday	Wednesday	Thursday	Friday	Weekly total tallies	Did I meet my weekly goal? Yes/No (If no, what is one action I am going to put in place for next week? What help do I need to meet my goal?)

School/Home Communication System

Student Name: _____

Parent name and contact: _____

Date: Time: Method of Contact: ☐ Phone ☐ Email ☐ Note Home ☐ Conference in Person ☐ Other: _____	Reason to contact:	Notes/Outcomes:
Date: Time: Method of Contact: ☐ Phone ☐ Email ☐ Note Home ☐ Conference in Person ☐ Other: _____	Reason to contact:	Notes/Outcomes:
Date: Time: Method of Contact: ☐ Phone ☐ Email ☐ Note Home ☐ Conference in Person ☐ Other: _____	Reason to contact:	Notes/Outcomes:

PBIS Behavior Expectations Matrix Review Form

Date and time of PBIS schoolwide matrix review (if behavior incident involves one location on the PBIS schoolwide matrix, that particular location's expectations and rules can be specifically assigned for review):

What are your school's school-wide behavior expectations? (If behavior incident involves one location on the PBIS schoolwide matrix, use that particular location's expectations and rules for this response.)

What behavior expectation, rule, and/or standard did you not meet? Why do you believe you did not meet this expectation?

What are the appropriate behaviors identified in the behavior matrix area you did not meet?

How will you demonstrate these identified appropriate behaviors?

What were you feeling when you engaged in the misbehavior?

Wrong Way, Right Way Elementary Form

Wrong Way	Right Way
How did you feel?	How do you think you would feel if you selected the right way?
What will you do next time?	
Student signature or initials:	

Classroom Agreement Review

What are our classroom agreements?

What is important to have classroom agreements?

Why is it important to have classroom agreements?

What part of the classroom agreement did you not follow?

What is your commitment in following through on the classroom agreement?

What support do you need to meet the classroom agreement expectations?

What can be a signal between you and the teacher to ensure the classroom agreement is being followed?

Review your responses with the teacher and include any additional notes summarizing what you and the teacher agreed on to ensure you are meeting the classroom agreement expectations. Please initial below and ask your teacher to initial so you are both on the same page.

Student initials: _____   Teacher initials: _____

Project-Based Behavior Learning Plan

Behavior Focus	Response
Context (understand the problem behavior)	
Guiding Question(s)	
Choice of Project	
21st Century Skill Being Addressed	
PBL Project Advisor (name and approval)	
Timeline for Completion	
Where or to Whom Will the Project Be Presented?	
Respond and Reflect (respond to the guiding questions)	
Sign-Off by PBL Advisor (date of completion)	

Parent/Educator/Administrator/Student Alternative Discipline Compact

Date: _____

Student name: _____ Administrator name: _____

Teacher or other educator stakeholder name: _____

Parent/guardian name: _____

Instructions: Complete the compact with stakeholders. Student is the lead of the compact. Student is required to collect the initials with support from all stakeholders.

Administrator Role in the alternative discipline:

•

Teacher or Other Identified Educator Stakeholder Role in the alternative discipline:

•

Parent/Guardian Role in the alternative discipline:

•

Student Role in the alternative discipline:

•

Compact Agreement Initials:

Student: _____ Administrator: _____ Teacher/Other: _____ Parent/Guardian: _____

*Check-In Initials: Initial if meeting your end of the agreement

Week 1

Student: _____ Administrator: _____ Teacher/Other: _____ Parent/Guardian: _____

Week 2

Student: _____ Administrator: _____ Teacher/Other: _____ Parent/Guardian: _____

Week 3

Student: _____ Administrator: _____ Teacher/Other: _____ Parent/Guardian: _____

Week 4

Student: _____ Administrator: _____ Teacher/Other: _____ Parent/Guardian: _____

Problem Behavior Decision Rule Form

Use the Decision Rule Form to serve as a flowchart that allows students to see visual representations of possible positive and negative outcomes stemming from their decisions. Feel free to add as many consequence boxes as you see necessary.

Decision:

Appropriate Behavior:

Inappropriate Behavior:

(+) Consequence:

(+) Consequence:

(−) Consequence:

(−) Consequence:

Commitment to Appropriate Behavior:

Huddle Process Form

A huddle is a quick check-in/reflection opportunity for the student with stakeholders during their alternative discipline contract. Student will participate in three check-in huddle sessions with at least two stakeholders, answering the following questions.

Huddle Guiding Questions:

1. What have you learned from the behavior incident?

2. What kind of impact has this behavior incident had on you? Others?

3. What have you learned based on what you have heard from others involved?

What are the huddle agreements?

What was the question based on the behavior incident we are huddling about?

What have I learned from this behavior incident?

Huddle session 1: With who/when? Question(s) discussed? Reflection?

Huddle session 2: With who/when? Question(s) discussed? Reflection?

Huddle session 3: With who/when? Question(s) discussed? Reflection?

Community Member Mentor Form

Select your community member mentor

Why did you select this mentor?

What did you discuss?

Check-in dates and signature

Recorded interview and reflection

Instructional Research Template

Name: _____ Date: _____

Instructions: Research your topic. Identify at least two key learnings around your topic area.

Describe your key learning (cite evidence):

_____

_____

_____

_____

_____

_____

_____

_____

Describe your key learning (cite evidence):

_____

_____

_____

_____

_____

_____

_____

_____

Getting to Know You Questionnaire

Your Name: _____ Other Student's Name: _____

Date: _____

Develop 10 questions you would like the other student to answer about themselves or the situation.

Developed Question	Student Response
1.	
2.	
3.	
4.	
5.	
6.	
7.	
8.	
9.	
10.	

Reflection after reviewing responses: What did you learn from this experience? How will you assure this student you will not engage in this type of behavior again?

Faculty/Staff Mentor Checklist

☐ Establish a relationship with the student

☐ Check in at least once a week

☐ Use data when having discussions with the student

☐ Help the student set goals

☐ Help teach student how to progress monitor set goals

☐ Log discussions

☐ Attend meetings and be a liaison for the student

☐ Reteach student essential skills needed to succeed

☐ Be consistent

Mentor Log

Student Name: _____

Mentor Name: _____

Date	Check-In Update on Specific Behavior What is going well? Explain.	Check-In Update on Specific Behavior What can improve? Explain.	Student Next Steps	Mentor Next Steps

Student Signature:_____ Mentor Signature:_____

Student Mentor Checklist

❏ Establish a relationship with the student or peer you are mentoring

❏ Check in with your student mentee at least weekly

❏ Give tips on how to make good decisions

❏ Celebrate the wins with the student or peer you are mentoring

Student Mentor Reflection Log

Student Mentor Name: _____

Student or Peer Mentee Name: _____

Date	Check-In Update on Specific Behavior What is going well for your mentee? Explain.	What tip(s) did you provide your mentee?	Reflection: Share a few sentences about how it is going with your mentee after each check-in.
Week 1 Check-In Date:			
Week 2 Check-In Date:			
Week 3 Check-In Date:			
Week 4 Check-In Date:			

Student Mentor Signature: _____

Dear Self Letter Template

Write a letter to yourself. Use the prompts to help you. Check in with a designated adult prior to school every morning for the next two weeks to read your letter to yourself.

Initial after reading each morning.

Day 1	Day 2	Day 3	Day 4	Day 5	Day 6	Day 7	Day 8	Day 9	Day 10

Dear _____,

I made a poor decision by _____

_____

_____

This decision does not define me. I am not a bad person. I want to learn from this decision by

_____

_____

I have committed to the following so I do not engage in this behavior again: _____

_____

_____

Some days are going to be harder than others. On hard days, I am going to remind myself to

_____

_____

I am going to ask for help on a bad day by _____

_____

_____

When I feel discouraged, I am going to tell myself _____

_____

_____

Sincerely,

Write "Your Narrative" Individual Contract

Who am I?

_____

_____

_____

_____

What are some poor choices I have made in the past at school (*my old narrative*)?

_____

_____

_____

_____

What do I want to see for myself (*my new narrative*) when it comes to behavior and academics in school?

_____

_____

_____

_____

How do I plan on making this *new narrative* come true?

_____

_____

_____

_____

(Continued)

(Continued)

What help do I need to make this *new narrative* come true?

_____

_____

_____

_____

Who will I reach out to and how often to help me make this *new narrative* come true?

_____

_____

_____

_____

What are my short-term goals toward this *new narrative*?

_____

_____

_____

_____

What are my long-term goals toward this *new narrative*?

_____

_____

_____

_____

My work toward *my new narrative* will begin on: _____

Student Signature of Commitment to *my new narrative:* _____

Check-in Commitment Schedule

Date _____ Check in with _____ Commitments _____ Initials: _____

Date _____ Check in with _____ Commitments _____ Initials: _____

Date _____ Check in with _____ Commitments _____ Initials: _____

Date _____ Check in with _____ Commitments _____ Initials: _____

Date _____ Check in with _____ Commitments _____ Initials: _____

Date _____ Check in with _____ Commitments _____ Initials: _____

Date _____ Check in with _____ Commitments _____ Initials: _____

Date _____ Check in with _____ Commitments _____ Initials: _____

Secondary Think Sheet

Student Name: _____

Date: _____

Period: _____

Describe the behavior(s) you demonstrated.

Was that behavior a good decision? Why or why not?

Who did you hurt?

What goal were you trying to accomplish?

Next time you have that goal, how will you meet it without hurting anybody? What behavior will you demonstrate instead?

Scenario Reflections Sheet

Scenario	Reflection
Sarah and Lori used to be best friends until they liked the same boy. Sarah did not like that Lori was talking to the boy so she called Lori names in front of all the other students.	
Jeff yelled at his teacher and walked out of the classroom when he was told to start his work.	
Jordan stole money from his teacher's desk.	
Zane refuses to dress for PE every day. He is disrespectful to his PE teacher. When the PE teacher reminds him about his grade, he tells the PE teacher he doesn't care if he gets an F in class.	
Add scenario:	
Add scenario:	
Add scenario:	

Student-Led Empathy Interview Template

Interview Date: _____ Interviewer: _____ Interviewee: _____

Step 1. CHECK-IN

Insert notes here about the interviewee:

Step 2. PURPOSE: Explain the purpose of the interview

Step 3. QUESTIONS: Sample questions: How did my behavior impact you? How did my behavior make you feel? Is there anything else you would like to share?

Log the question(s) asked and response(s) below:

Question posed:

Interviewee Response:

Question posed:

Interviewee Response:

Question posed:

Interviewee Response:

Question posed:

Interviewee Response:

Step 4. WRAP-UP: Thank them, wrap up and validate their input, and set up a follow-up to share the actions taken as a result of their input.

Validation statements:

I heard you share . . .

I heard you share . . .

I heard you share . . .

Schedule a follow-up interview to share the actions taken as a result of their input: Follow-up interview date: _____

Behavior Streak Sheet

Streak Focus Behavior: _____

Goal/Reinforcement: _____

_____

_____

Example: Every three consecutive (Yes) days, student receives a student choice reinforcement (i.e., free homework pass). The streak reinforcement goals can be adjusted based on the needs of the individual student (i.e., hourly, daily, weekly).

Did I keep my streak?: Insert the corresponding image daily.

💧	Yes
⏳	No (One occurrence triggers a one-on-one chat with teacher to help student get the streak restarted)
★	Indicates streak reinforcement

Week of:					Week of:				

Week of:					Week of:				

Week of:					Week of:				

Week of:					Week of:				

Belonging Exercise

Step 1: Student completes Student Belonging Self-Assessment: Student Version

Student Belonging Self-Assessment: Student Version

1. Tell me about a time when you felt like you belonged in school.

   a. How did that feel?

   b. What did you experience?

   c. What made you feel like you belonged?

   d. Can you give an example of an experience that made you feel like you belonged?

2. Tell me about a time when you felt like you belonged in a classroom.

   a. How did that feel?

   b. What made you feel like you belonged?

   c. Can you give an example of an experience that made you feel like you belonged?

3. Is there an adult or adults on campus you feel connected to?

4. Do your teachers believe in you?

(Continued)

(Continued)

Step 2: Teacher completes Student Belonging Self-Assessment: Teacher Version

Student Belonging Self-Assessment: Teacher Version

1. Do you believe the student feels like they belong in your classroom?

2. Do you feel like you are an adult on campus the student feels like they can go to?

3. Do you believe the student feels like you believe in them?

4. Do you feel like the student feels connected in school?

Is there a disconnect between the student and teacher responses? What are some ways we can help bring alignment to how the student feels?

Student Contract

Student: _____

Focus Behavior:_____

Goal: _____

Date	Mon	Tues	Wed	Thurs	Fri
A.M. to Recess					
Recess to Lunch					
Lunch and Lunch Recess					
After Lunch Recess to the End of School					

___ 's = Daily Reward _____

___ 's = Friday Reward _____

Parent's Signature: _____ Date: _____

PART IV

Bringing It All Together

(Alternative Discipline Contract)

8

So What Now?

You have been given a lot of information to process in this book. Do not feel overwhelmed at this point. Challenge yourself to use the alternative discipline framework as a guide to assign meaningful discipline. For educators who are ready to take this step, you will see a difference in how you work with students after the first time you successfully assign discipline this way. As educators, we have a moral imperative to reach *all* students academically and behaviorally. Our school/district mission and vision statements *say* all students, but do our actions support it? Sending a student home repeatedly for behavior certainly doesn't support these statements. We understand using discipline as a teaching opportunity to change behavior will feel awkward at first, but isn't this the case for any new educational practices? You must be willing to evolve every day (not just in words, but actions) to keep up with the increasingly complex and challenging needs of our students.

As you begin this journey, ask yourself the following reflective questions:

1. Do you believe in doing discipline in this way?

2. Is creating and maintaining a solid foundational behavior system at your school a priority?

3. Are you willing to allocate time and resources to this method of discipline?

4. Have you analyzed your school discipline data for disproportionality for underserved populations?

5. Are you ready for challenging, courageous conversations?

6. Are you ready to save lives?

ALTERNATIVE DISCIPLINE CONTRACT

The Alternative Discipline Contract is a template to ensure you are applying all components of our alternative discipline framework (i.e., at least one restorative, one reflective, and one instructional). However, you may have two restorative, one reflective, and three instructional and that is okay. Be aware some alternative discipline components may be happening concurrently to each other. The order in which they are written on the contract does not necessarily indicate the order it must take place. For example, with a restorative component, a student may need to calm down and reflect prior to authentically completing the restorative portion of their contract.

Use this template as a graphic organizer to plan and implement the alternative discipline contracts. Use the menu of alternatives and the additional universal alternative discipline forms and processes in this book as a guide to select each appropriate response for your student's alternative discipline contract. Typically, the alternative discipline contract is led and assigned by a school administrator with stakeholder input.

We also added a section to the alternative discipline contract to include how a student can earn privileges back as a result of the completion of the components in the alternative discipline contract. We want to reiterate that students are on this contract in lieu of a suspension. The completion of the contract will help restore the confidence from the teacher, administration, and others. As the student demonstrates progress, they will begin to earn privileges back. We want to make the connection to real-life consequences; when adults engage in these types of behaviors, trust is broken and privileges are taken away.

Alternative Discipline Contract

Student Name: _____

Assigning Administrator(s): _____

Beginning Date: _____

Behavior Description:

_____

_____

_____

_____

Perceived Function of the Behavior:

_____

_____

_____

_____

Components of the Alternative Discipline	Responsible Person(s)	Date to Be Completed By	Component Completed: Yes or No
Component 1:			
Component 2:			
Component 3:			
Component 4:			
Component 5:			

What part of the consequence is restorative?

_____

_____

_____

_____

What part of the consequence is reflective?

_____

_____

_____

_____

What part of the consequence is instructional?

_____

_____

_____

_____

What privileges will the student earn back as a result of completion of this Alternative Discipline Contract (timeline)?

_____

_____

_____

_____

Additional comments or notes:

_____

_____

_____

_____

_____

_____

Student Signature: _____

Administrator Signature: _____

Other Signature: _____

ALTERNATIVE DISCIPLINE STUDENT INPUT FORM

Use the following Alternative Discipline Student Input Form to allow for student voice and agency in the alternative discipline. The student is also part of their alternative discipline process, so—when appropriate—allowing their input in this process can result in additional ownership of their behavior. Note: Let the student know their input will be considered in the development of their contract. Some students will surprise you and have very thoughtful responses that are better than anything we could have created; others, however, will need very structured facilitation of this form.

Alternative Discipline Student Input Form

Name: _____

Grade: _____

What was the problem behavior you were engaged in?

Why do you believe you engaged in this behavior?

Who do you believe your behavior impacted? List and explain how your behavior impacted them.

Who: _____ Behavior Impact: _____

Who: _____ Behavior Impact: _____

Who: _____ Behavior Impact: _____

Who: _____ Behavior Impact: _____

Restorative Component

What does restoring a relationship based on your behavior mean to you?

How does that apply to this incident?

What can you do to restore these relationships?

(Continued)

(Continued)

To whom will you need to restore? How? And by when?

I need to restore with _____ by _____ by _____.

I need to restore with _____ by _____ by _____.

I need to restore with _____ by _____ by _____.

I need to restore with _____ by _____ by _____.

Reflective Component

What does reflecting on this experience mean to you?

How does that apply to this incident?

How can you reflect on this behavior?

Instructional Component

What does learning from your mistake (instructional) mean to you?

How does that apply to this incident?

What can you do that is instructional?

[ ]

Alternative Discipline (all components)

What do you believe your Alternative Discipline Contract should entail?

[ ]

My restorative component will include

[ ]

My reflective component will include

[ ]

My instructional component will include

[ ]

What privileges will I be working toward as I am completing my Alternative Discipline Contract?

[ ]

Who is an adult at the school you feel can help you learn from the behavior incident and help you with your Alternative Discipline Contract?

[ ]

Student Signature: _____

CHALLENGE TO EDUCATORS

We challenge educators to go above and beyond when addressing student behavior. A student's brain is not fully developed until early adulthood; they will make mistakes and need support from adults to help learn from those mistakes. We as educators must teach them how to act, how to make good decisions, and to succeed in the real world. We cannot expect this to happen while not supporting a student's social-emotional development. We cannot guarantee *all* students the opportunity to learn and grow using punitive, exclusionary contexts. Follow the guidelines provided in this book and invest with sincere commitment, and you will see what we refer to as the "Art of Discipline."

I commit to using alternative discipline in my school or district by:

_____

_____

_____

_____

_____

After using this approach, I found that:

_____

_____

_____

_____

_____

References

Balfanz, R., & Boccanfuso, C. (2007). *Falling off the path to graduation: Early indicators brief.* Graduates Center.

Balfanz, R., & Fox, J. (2014). Sent home and put off-track: The antecedents, disproportionalities, and consequences of being suspended in the ninth grade. *Journal of Applied Research on Children: Informing Policy for Children at Risk, 5*(2), 13.

Breslow, J. M. (2012). By the numbers: Dropping out of high school. *Frontline: Dropout Nation.* https://www.pbs.org/wgbh/frontline/article/by-the-numbers-dropping-out-of-high-school/

Chard, D., Smith, S., & Sugai, G. (1992). Packaged discipline programs: A consumer's guide. In J. Marr & G. Tindal (Eds.), *1992 Oregon conference monograph* (pp. 19–27). University of Oregon.

Hannigan, J. D., & Hannigan, J. (2018a). *The PBIS tier three handbook: A practical approach to implementing the champion model.* Corwin Press.

Hannigan, J. D., & Hannigan, J. (2018b). *The PBIS tier two handbook: A practical approach to implementing the champion model.* Corwin Press.

Hannigan, J., Hannigan, J. D., Mattos, M., & Buffum, A. (2020). *Behavior solutions: Teaching academic and social skills through RTI at Work.* Solution Tree.

Hannigan, J., & Hauser, L. (2014). *The PBIS tier one handbook: A practical approach to implementing the champion model.* Corwin.

Hanson, K., & Stipek, D. (2014). *School v prisons: Education's the way to cut prison population.* Stanford Graduate School of Education. https://ed.stanford.edu/in-the-media/schools-v-prisons-educations-way-cut-prison-population-op-ed-deborah-stipek

Hattie, J. (2018, October). *Visible Learning plus 250+ influences on student achievement.* Retrieved from https://us.corwin.com/sites/default/files/250_influences_10.1.2018.pdf

Irvin, L. K., Tobin, T. J., Sprague, J. R., Sugai, G., & Vincent, C. G. (2004). Validity of office discipline referral measures as indices of school-wide behavioral status and effects of school-wide behavioral interventions. *Journal of Positive Behavior Interventions, 6*(3), 131–147.

Leone, P. E., Christle, C. A., Nelson, M., Skiba, R., Frey, A., & Jolivette, K. (2003). *School failure, race, and disability: Promoting positive outcomes, decreasing vulnerability for involvement with the juvenile delinquency system.* The National Center on Education, Disability, and Juvenile Justice.

Losen, D. J. (2011). *Discipline policies, successful schools, and racial justice.* National Education Policy Center, School of Education, University of Colorado Boulder.

Losen, D. J., & Martin, K. (2018). The unequal impact of suspension on the opportunity to learn in California. *Civil Rights Project-Proyecto Derechos Civiles.*

Mayer, G. R. (1995). Preventing antisocial behavior in the schools. *Journal of Applied Behavior Analysis, 28*(4), 467–478.

McCook, J. E. (2006). *The RTI guide: Developing and implementing a model in your schools*. LRP Publications.

OECD. (2014). *Education at a glance 2014: OECD Indicators*. OECD Publishing. https://doi.org/10.1787/eag-2014-en or https://www.oecd.org/education/Education-at-a-Glance-2014.pdf

Perry, B. L., & Morris, E. W. (2014). Suspending progress: Collateral consequences of exclusionary punishment in public schools. *American Sociological Review, 79*(6). https://doi.org/0003122414556308

Rumberger, R. W., & Losen, D. J. (2017). The hidden costs of California's harsh school discipline: And the localized economic benefits from suspending fewer high school students. *Civil Rights Project-Proyecto Derechos Civiles*.

Skiba, R., & Peterson, R. (1999). The dark side of zero tolerance: Can punishment lead to safe schools? *Phi Delta Kappan, 8*(5), 372–382.

Skiba, R. J., & Rausch, M. K. (2006). Zero tolerance, suspension, and expulsion: Questions of equity and effectiveness. In C. M. Evertson & C. S. Weinstein (Eds.), *Handbook of classroom management: Research, practice, and contemporary issues* (pp. 1063–1089). Lawrence Erlbaum Associates Publishers.

Tavernise, S. (2012, February 9). Education gap grows between rich and poor, studies say. *The New York Times*. www.nytimes.com/2012/02/10/education/education-gap-grows-between-rich-and-poor-studies-show.html?_r=1&nl=todaysheadlines&emc=tha2

Todd, A. W., Campbell, A. L., Meyer, G. G., & Horner, R. H. (2008). The effects of a targeted intervention to reduce problem behaviors: Elementary school implementation of check in—check out. *Journal of Positive Behavior Interventions, 10*(1), 46–55.

Wald, J., & Losen, D. (2003). *Deconstructing the school-to-prison pipeline: New directions for youth development*. Jossey-Bass.

U.S. Department of Education Office for Civil Rights. (2014). Civil rights data collection data snapshot: School discipline. *Issue brief no. 1*.

Index

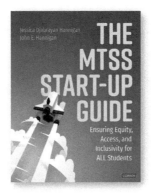
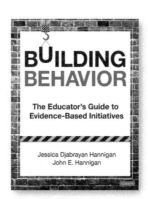

CORWIN
A SAGE Publishing Company

Helping educators make the greatest impact

CORWIN HAS ONE MISSION: to enhance education through intentional professional learning.

We build long-term relationships with our authors, educators, clients, and associations who partner with us to develop and continuously improve the best evidence-based practices that establish and support lifelong learning.